NATURE,
ART
AND FLOWER
ARRANGEMENT

Frontispiece:
In a unified composition, wood carvings by Anri of Italy, plants from Nature, and the flower arrangers art combine to illustrate the theme of the book.

Arranger: Mrs. Howard McClelland
Photographer: Ricci Studio

NATURE, ART AND FLOWER ARRANGEMENT

by Emma Hodkinson Cyphers

 *published by*

Hearthside Press, Inc.
New York

When Nature gives a gorgeous rose,
Or yields the simplest fern,
She puts this legend on every leaf:
To whom it may concern.

JOHN G. SAXE

CONTENTS

PREFACE

Another book on flower arrangement? Yes, but this is not a "how-to-do-it" in the usual sense. Rather it explores the creative possibilities which are neglected in most flower arrangement volumes. Few contemporary arrangers fully realize that excitingly creative designs go hand in hand with observation.

To observe, of course, is to see, but not by the eyes alone; seeing is the culmination of all senses. To see is an unprovable part of living for you see not only what things are, but what *you* are, what you *think*, what you *feel*. What we see is no more and no less than what we are.

From such observation comes inspiration, the creative impulse. It is, perhaps, the most elusive feature in a work of art, yet its source is everywhere. Nature so rich and varied is an inexhaustible stimulant to mind, heart, and imagination, and in *Nature, Art, and Flower Arrangement* we go to her for inspiration. Thus the arranger finds kinship with all the fine arts, for all are related through Nature.

NATURE IS NOT ART

The laws of Nature are basic to art. Indeed, even though these basic principles have been used differently through the ages, it is because they are fundamental to life that we can respond to the artistic expression of

7

any people, anywhere, and in all periods throughout history. But we must recognize that art is only the image of cosmic order. I mean to say Nature is not art, for Nature represents inborn character while art, a product of man, is a result of planning. Art, therefore, is an *activity*—the making or doing of something.

Goethe, the German poet, proclaimed that art is extension of Nature with the simile of root and branch to which we can hold today. We might say that where Nature stops the artist begins, using principles of Nature to create art forms. Her thrusts and stresses, for instance, are applied in architecture. The cantilevering principle on which is built "Falling Waters" at Bear Run, Pennsylvania, is an example. Principles of atmospheric light and color are used as in impressionist paintings, or the earlier atmospheric paintings: those of Ryder who brought the mist of the sea to his canvas as no other artist could; of Turner with poetic renderings of natural phenomenon such as a snowstorm; of Whistler who excelled in conveying the twilight hours in his Nocturnes. Proportions of the human body based on hand and finger length are seen in Leonardo's drawings, and in Greek sculpture of an earlier period. Even the motions of Nature—her falling leaves, for instance—are extended into art forms of which Calder's early mobiles are superb examples.

Throughout this book the term Nature is used in its most common sense of organic flora and fauna and inorganic elements of land, water, sky, light, and atmosphere which can be perceived by the senses. But all this is only a fraction of our greater concern with Nature—that is, the oneness of Nature and man. Aristotle felt it as a profound relationship between man's soul and the rhythmic harmony of Nature. For Leonardo, this unity was the human body likened to the universe. Soil, he said, was the flesh, water the blood, bones the rock, and air the spirit. As for me, in looking for the meaning of design on the face of Nature, I cannot help but speculate on the meaning of life as well; I have experienced in Nature some of the deepest truths. Thus Nature links itself with daily living.

PRELUDE TO CREATIVE WORK

The study of this book reveals that Nature contains all elements of all design as a keyboard contains all notes of all music. To know her internal as well as external qualities brings awareness of the relationship between creativity and man's personality. This will involve the arranger with an instinctive urgency to communicate personal insights through more creative arrangement forms.

This brings us to what I wish to stress in these introductory remarks: We must not take Nature for granted. To be worthy of her we must approach her clothed with humility and reverence. John Taylor Arms, the American etcher, urged that when we look at Nature we should empty our minds of useless things, of ugly things; for the eye cannot see what it looks upon unless the heart and mind are in accord. To the modest eye, even the beauty of a weed will demand respect for with humanity it obeys the same underlying laws.

THEME AND SUBSTANCE OF THIS BOOK

The aim of this volume is to familiarize you with Nature's designs and methods. It is offered with the hope that it will be provocative to fellow arrangers.

I NATURE, MAN'S ETERNAL INSPIRATION

It is through Nature that mankind is fed not only physically but spiritually. She is the great initiator in religions, in philosophies, and in the arts. Undeniably, she has always kindled man's mind and guided his hand. Who is unaware of resemblance between the silhouette of the pagoda and the shape of the native pine of the Orient, the Egyptian column and the lotus plant of the Nile, the famed tower of Pisa and the horsetail *(Equisatum)*, an ancient evergreen? And here in America, Frank Lloyd Wright's response in architecture to the involute of a Nautilus shell is manifested in the Guggenheim Museum in New York.

What peculiar and persistent intuition, enduring through all time, has caused artists always to stay close to Nature? Is it that natural form and color arouse fundamental sensitivities of the human eye and imagination? It is known that man enjoys the familiar—could it be that Nature beckons because it is near at hand?

Nature's hold on man are these to be sure, but there is more—a deeper thing. Perhaps unconsciously, but inevitably, man feels the same creative forces as those in Nature. The combination of elements so that each functions its unqualified best and each relates in form and substance to a vital whole is art. And too, it is Nature.

10

Plate 1   For the interior of the Guggenheim museum, architect Frank Lloyd Wright found inspiration in the many-chambered, spiral shell of the nautilus.

Courtesy of
   The Solomon R. Guggenheim
   Museum, New York

NATURE AND MANKIND

It is written in the Book of Life that Nature and life are inseparable, and man an inescapable part. In God's Creation a successively higher plane of life on this planet culminated in the human being, created to use the natural things in the physical world around him. And indeed, problems of survival made this not a matter of choice, but of necessity. Illuminating pages of history teach that environment is the most prevailing and powerful influence in life.

The need for food obliged Palaeolithic man to fashion implements for hunting and fishing from bone and stone; thus he became the first craftsman. Man lived so close to Nature that he associated even these tools of existence with plant life around him, his "willow-knife," for instance. Today, are we so very different? Even though the history of art does not support the idea, who among us has not associated the pillars and vaulting ribs of great Gothic cathedrals with forest aisles? And does not the Gothic spire seem the equivalent to the Lombardy poplar with its growth structure pointing heavenward? And has not an airplane aloft in space and riding the billows, been likened to a huge bird shearing the clouds with ease and smoothness?

PRIMAL URGE A FORCE

In searching out the origins of design, we discover two distinct ways in which Nature has been an initial force in art's progress. One, and probably the most influential, is the inherent need to create.

Harking back to the very youth of humanity, the drive to find something to divert man from monotonous routine was as strong as the need for food. This was manifested in the use of sponges, shells, fish vertebrae, teeth and claws of animals, pebbles, bits of ivory for self-adornment. It is a fact that a first creation by man was a necklace of such items strung together. Its planned design was response to man's intuitive impulse to find order, to identify himself with the balance, proportion, and rhythm of the natural world.

The second, and perhaps the more fascinating factor in Nature's influence on art, was primitive man's deep urge to deify Nature as the source of his life. Man saw the sea at sunrise and sunset, the valley in the moonlight, and felt his heart surge in awe and wonder, even as you and I. His unconscious, but nevertheless insatiable yearning for the divine is a common goal of man. He brought this to fruit in worship; no primitive group was without some form of worship. A belief in life after death, no matter how crude, became an important aspect of his religious sense. Living against the enchanting background of Nature, early man literally "walked in beauty" throughout his life, so it is not surprising that Nature was interwoven with his idea of eternity. To man, a thinking creature, those things which enhanced his physical body would surely please his spirit in a life beyond. Archaeologist excavations of burial graves have revealed the trinkets with which on earth he beautified himself.

Burial treasures of later periods were conventionalized or naturalistic leaves, flowers, fruits and seed pods fashioned from stone or gold. These show growth in aesthetic development, but more important, they emphasize the interrelationship of man and Nature.

NATURAL FORCES REVERED

Because in remote antiquity there was no knowledge of the laws of the universe, people were unable to understand natural phenomena. Thunder, lightning, floods were out of the ordinary, so they were happenings to be feared. This induced primitive man to venerate natural forces as gods and goddesses; to create images in their honor. It was inevitable that from the worship of natural phenomena, glorification of all things in Nature would develop.

Vegetable life was especially revered because it sustained all other life. In time, plants took on ritual meaning. To carry them in sacred processional ceremony became a favored attraction in religious festivals of the Graeco-Roman epoch. We can see today evidence of this ancient reverence for that which sprang from the earth in sculptured likenesses on walls of temple ruins. As civilization progressed, man came to know that while natural panorama reveals the presence of a Supreme Creator, Nature cannot be a substitute for God. With the passing of paganism, the plants so endeared to the hearts of men were accepted as religious symbols in the early Christian Church.

LAWS OF ORDER

It is to the Greek philosophers that cosmic order first became a conscious realization. With the advent of science it was the quest for truth that found everying in Nature a part of an integrated whole, and that natural order, a matter of universal laws, controls all Nature, including man. With the spirit of man and Nature thought of as one, man recognized the spiritual dimension of Nature which can invoke strong emotional experience in the human heart. Beethoven conveyed emotional experience when he penned, "Every tree seems to say 'Holy, Holy.'" And Britain's author, Belloc, spoke the same voice when he talked of "those magnificent creatures of God . . . the Alps."

ART ROOTS IN NATURE

But what has this to do with Nature as eternal inspiration for artists? Like man himself, his artistic endeavors have roots in Nature. Is it not conceivable that when man understood the vital relationship between himself and his natural surroundings that Nature became for him not only a source of existence, of self beautification, of worship, but of art as well? Indeed, Nature seems to fuse so easily into art. Both, as symbols of beauty, of well being, refresh the spirit.

In his creative impulse the ancients turned always to Nature for inspiration and guidance, imposing the forms of Nature upon their art.

For eternity and for splendor the Pharaohs in Egypt built their pyramids to echo majestic mountains which time had not destroyed. And from the shape of the sage of the Holy Land, Hebrews evolved a seven-branched candelabrum of religious and artistic significance. The ancient Chinese civilization created artistic vases and bowls in the forms of gourds and lotus flowers. And in the New World the light of excavations has shown that prehistoric craftsmen found Nature a fertile incentive for the shapes of water-carrying jugs and other practical objects.

Now, if primitive man inflicted the forms of Nature on his art, he also inflicted his art on Nature, for he embellished religious objects with decorative patterns of lines and shapes he interpreted as symbols of things he saw in Nature. Among them were the spiral of the shell and whirlpool, the circle of the sun and full moon, the crescent of the new moon and rainbow, the scallop of rolling hills, the zigzag of sharp mountain crags and lightning, the compound curves of flame, and the straight lines of the vertical tree trunk, the horizontal horizon, and the slanting rain. And our American Indians decorated, as they do today, with motifs derived from animals as well as plants. Because man is endowed with an instinct for seeking repetition, it is logical that these earliest decorative patterns distributed the symbols in a simple harmony of repetition—a harmony in natural things with which he felt a sympathy. The strata of Nature's rock are revelatory.

Man's aesthetic sense developed when he realized that even though Nature abounds in repetitious pattern and form, she plays variations upon them. With increasing ability to respond to this, man lifted himself above instinct, and art progressed. Although repetition remained the basis of order for ancient man, repetition plus variety became, and remains for us today, the ultimate in design. Thus man kept his vision fresh.

This attainment demonstrates that laws which produce natural structure also determine art form; the law of Nature is the root which nourishes art as, from its root, a tree draws nourishment.

TIMELESS DESIGN

Form and plan in the physical world transcend time and place. A reason, surely, is their great beauty—not a beauty that appeals to one generation and is considered old-fashioned in the next; not just a beauty accepted by one nation, one race, and rejected by all others, but a beauty that is without boundary in time, and is of universal appeal. Can we deny that universal appreciation is anything other than fundamental instinct?

There can be no monotony in nature-inspired art for although appreciation of Nature's beauty is basic, there is variety in its meaning for man. One artist may find his wellspring in the heavy and dynamic energy of hills or rocky formations which forever underlie the green of life, or he may thrill most particularly to the lure of open valley and plain. The procreative urge for another may find support in delicate or moving structures, or in the mystery of suspended life in the root, the seed, the egg that await another spring. The privilege of personal selection from Nature's ineffable beauty adds sparkle to the form or pattern that fires an individual's creative imagination into activity. Some brush her moods on canvas, shape her forms in sculpture, chisel her patterns in wood; others describe her beauty on the printed page, or in music, or with flowers.

Art is, indeed, in a continuous flux, but all along the trail of long centuries Nature has been the guidepost directing man's creative imagination, and it is Nature, undeniably Nature, that is the unifying element in works which differ in style and in conception. Principles of design inculcated by ancient nations still are, and always will be, a part of all art, for the Nature of the past, their source, is now the Nature of the present, and is ever the Nature of the future.

NEW HORIZONS FOR ARRANGERS

For the arranger the natural world can provide the most meaningful of aesthetic experiences. Nature offers a perpetual and valid touchstone but without freshness of form, design becomes weak and ineffective, liable to mediocrity. I am not suggesting that we disregard past values, but simply that we adjust our outlook to new horizons. If the arrangement art is to improve as well as change, it must grow from the primary root of all great art—Nature and the individual.

Among artists, the arranger has a unique privilege for he works with the products of Nature. How logical then to study arrangement in relation to Nature rather than apart from her. Let us, then, go forth into the out-of-doors and read Nature's teachings.

II SIGHT AND INSIGHT

PERCEPTUAL VISION

Nature's beauty is made up of simple things—a tree, a hill, a bird flying along with the advance of clouds. Human artistry has produced nothing comparable to the wild loveliness of surf pushing against great rocky cliffs, or to equal the splendor of a leaf's intricate veining, or to rival the magnificence of moonlight filtered through white bracts along horizontally spread branches of a dogwood tree. Man thrills at delicate patterns in lace designed by Venetian weavers, but is apt to ignore the exquisite detail in the cap of the royal meadow flower of the carrot family, Queen Anne's Lace.

My own awakening to Nature began in the summer months of my childhood at Century Oak, my parents' country home in Pennsylvania. It was here that I first became aware of her subtleties—the sweeping curve of a tree branch, the veining of leaves, the gradation in a bird's wing, the fascination of sunlit pattern, the unique tracery of exposed roots along a woodland path. Long walks with my father to identify flora and fauna are cherished in memory and a resource of experience from which I can draw inspiration.

As a small girl I had a squirrellike fondness for collecting. Acorns were surely fairy chalices! A tiny lichen-lined nest eighteen feet above the

16

ground abandoned by a little jewel-colored hummingbird was, perhaps, a fairy bed! Iridescent feathers from the chicken house, occasional gems from the magnificent peacock's tail, and always the weird cases from which the cicada nymphs had emerged were part of my collection. A peak of thrill was a fern-imprinted fossil found in a woodland chamber.

In winter my mother's "curio cabinet," a case of wonders, gave pleasure to my inquisitive eye. The items which captivated me the most were from Nature. Among them was a small, dried, serpentine seahorse, as fragile as a butterfly. To me it was some mythical creature with its horse-like head and its spiralled tail like an unfolding fern yet somehow suggesting a coiled trunk of a miniature elephant. Then there was a sand-dollar, the dried, pale shell of a sea urchin with a five-petaled "flower" etched on its thin flat surface. And I recall the fingered sponge which looked for all the world like a cluster of classic-shaped vases. There was a bit of petrified wood from Arizona's Petrified Forest, its polished surface revealing beautiful color and design. I remember as though it were yesterday my excitement when a chunk of amethyst quartz with violet to purple hexagonal crystals came to rest beside it on the shelf. Later a fragment from the massive Percé Rock off Canada's Gaspé Peninsula, like translucent rock candy embedded in an opaque sand-colored quartz, brought still another thrill. Perhaps the most fascinating of all was a book of pressed seaweeds differing in design and color, between covers of slightly convex sea shells polished to a high luster.

It brought me pleasure to learn something about the strange and beautiful creations which fascinated me and aroused my imagination; I have enjoyed my will-o'-the-wisp trail of study ever since, and also, I might add, my urge to collect! There is something irresistible in the shapes and textures of such things as shells, stones, tree knots, and bits of roots. Occasionally a vague resemblance to animal or plant life attracts me, but usually it is the thing itself that prompts me to pick it up and turn it in my hand for better examination, and then add it to my collection to be used sometime in arrangement.

All these are mind conditioners derived from *perceptual* vision, a conscious sight of the actual thing before you. Such is purely objective seeing, with the subject, like a photographic likeness, appearing the same to all—a mere sensation of the optic nerve. Many go through life seeing only in this manner, but there is a keener way. This is through insight, an unconscious view which we term *conceptual* vision—that is, seeing by means of feeling or mental impression.

CONCEPTUAL VISION

Conceptual vision is completely subjective—seeing attentively with an "inner eye" which senses things. This is perceiving deeply, being aware of subtle implications that take on significance. The rose attracts the eye of most everyone, but only those who look deeply behold the velvet of its petals, a texture more exquisite than the velvet of a monarch's robe. You may know the yellow buttercup of the sunny field, but have you discovered the waxlike lacquer of the flower so like a tiny cup to catch the sunlight? No doubt you can distinguish between a weeping willow and a lordly oak tree, but do you sense the delicate and pendant inter- lacing lines of the one, the powerful vigor of the other? To a penetrating vision some trees appear to crouch while others seem ready to take wing.

Because of certain qualities the character of a locale takes on for most persons the same general associations, but to the eye that sees deeply, the overall impression will be a personal reaction. In a place generally thought of as quiet, for instance, you may feel relaxation, another may experience boredom.

Conceptual vision, then, is looking inward to discover the unusual about the familiar, of getting below the surface of things to become aware of their significance to *you*. In this personal relationship, seeing is refined; "I know *what* I like" becomes, "I know *why* I like." Deep seeing is a way of feeling, for always it comes from within.

A KEY TO CREATIVE WORK

The refined seeing of conceptual vision is the key to creative work for it depends on intellect, emotion, spirit, the whole of man. In deep perception, one's past experiences as well as all the senses are brought into play. If this were not so why would a patch of purple violets set my particular feelings astir? Is it the softness of color, the tenderness of the violets' texture? These factors have their influence but it is nostalgia that moves me more deeply. A spread of violets takes me back to Maytime in my childhood—to the pleasure of gathering in woodland haunts these divinities of beauty to carry home to my mother.

Plate 2   Feeling the rhythm and character of mountains painted in white and grays on a white silk wall scroll, the arranger has repeated their jagged peaks; the barren branches echo the mood of the bleakness in the winter scene . . . thus perception and conception produce inspired composition.

Arranger: Mrs. Raymond Russ Stoltz
Photographer: William Sevecke

Perhaps it is the form of a rock that will carry you back in memory to some object or incident. Trees, hills, clouds may give you a picture of scenic beauty, but your imagination and remembrance of a long-past experience may invest a landscape with emotional significance. A sunset is a natural phenomenon. It looks the same to all when viewed objectively —that is, when nothing but surface aspect is seen. But your mind, your heart, your imagination—conditions within your being—can color the view so you see it subjectively; it is penetrating vision which causes you to react personally.

SUMMATION

Conceptual vision is a matter of insight developed through awareness. One is truly creative when he animates his work with personal meaning of things resulting from the ability to see their inner nature in relation to his human character. Thus creation is a point of view. The creative artist stores images in his mind which may later affect his conceptual or inner vision. In fact some designers are more creative than others simply because they perceive more deeply; tucked away in their unconscious mind are impressions which can be drawn on when a need arises. Take time to perceive deeply for this is the key to creative work. It opens doors which enable everyone to reason logically, to apprehend intuitively, and to appreciate beauty to the full.

TO CULTIVATE DEEP SEEING

Few are destined to be great artists, but everyone has something of the artist within him; he is born with an urge to create. Awareness is possessed by every child, but unfortunately in the growing-up process, many fail to exercise this birthright, and natural sensitivity, like an unused muscle, shrivels and dies. Though suppressed in one's intellectual development, awareness, the servant of creativity, is innate and can be nurtured. To cultivate a habit of deep seeing, make an *adventure* of looking. Train yourself to see not only the obvious manifestations of beauty, like a cardinal's splash of red against winter's snow, but the more subtle show of beauty as jadelike luster of certain leaves in sunlight, the silvery sheen of wind-swept poplars, the gracefully scalloped flight of the bright little goldfinch in his sun-yellow and ebony plumage. To

Plate 3   A well-designed arrangement is seldom an accident. Here a dominance of smooth texture is suited to bold line and shape. On the right, to emphasize force of the elongated figure by contrast, is a curve of strelitzia foliage approximating a parabola of strength and tension.

Arranger: Mrs. A. R. Merrill
Photographer: Ellsworth

be aware, *looking* must be informed perception. We must determine why something has occult attraction, why the objects in combination fascinate with a definite sensation. We must note how things look from above, from below, in profile as well. How things appear under different circumstances, at different times of the day, involves important variables. Examine objects in varied light. See the color when things are young, when old, when dry, when wet. Notice too how something in relation to its surrounding appears quite different when we see it in another setting.

WHAT TO LOOK FOR

And so we agree that to create one must learn to see deeply; sensibilities that have become clogged or blunted must be cleared. But first one must know what to look for. Nature will not come to you; you must go to her—that is, you must put yourself in communication with her.

Plate 4   Here the thinking process is portrayed as if it were just being born—the twisted body and the tension in the muscles, expressing pain and difficulty.

The Thinker by Auguste Rodin (Bronze statuette)

Courtesy of The Metropolitan Museum of Art, New York
Gift of Thomas F. Ryan, 1910

To start, guard against the human tendency to see only those things which correspond with your own special interests. Two men walk the country road together. One, a naturalist, sees the trees, grasses, flowers, birds and other wild life. The other, an architect, sees the houses, barns, silos. In the woods a scientist will miss the subtlety of color tone so clearly visible to the painting artist. The American philosopher, Ralph Waldo Emerson, has written: "The difference between landscape and landscape is small, but there is great difference in the beholder."

So opening the heart and mind to what the eye rests upon is largely a matter of self-discipline. Much of the text in Nature's book is written in fine print; reading it trains the eye to see beyond the surface. Let us not be guilty of having the kind of lazy intellect which could provoke a comment such as the following to the painter, "Why Mr. Turner, I never saw any such light and color in Nature as you put on your canvas." If we condition our vision perhaps we too could reply, "Don't you wish you could; as for me, I never can hope to match with pigment the glory I see in the sky."

To prevent aimless looking, give purpose to the adventure. Consider one thing at a time—one aspect, one element, one principle in the spectacle you view. To more fully explain, let the subject of your looking be less important than effect, such, perhaps, as the way light falls on it revealing unique pattern or form. As simple a thing as this may be all that is required to gain a personal conception of a common sight, an idea for some future arrangement.

WHERE AND HOW TO BEGIN

Not only must we know *what* to look for in training the eye, but *where* and *how* to begin as well. It is not necessary to search out the picturesque landscape, for Nature spreads her patterns everywhere to be absorbed by appraising eyes and a recording mind. Your adventure can begin outside your own door. Examine organic lines of growing plants, the veining of leaves, the format and grouping of petals, and the color! Discrimination may be quickened by such simple practice as discovering how many kinds of green are represented; it is doubtful that you'll find

Plate 5   The theme "thinking" is present here too—but how different in mood from Plate 4. The composition is quiet and gentle. An Oriental figure nestles into a crevice formed by weathered wood. Behind and above the figure, a palm spathe inserted in wood adds dignity and depth; bark from a decayed tree stabilizes and determines width. The curled ends serve as little whirlpools of interest but at the same time nudge the eye toward the figure, keeping us aware of this which sets the mood. By using quiet tones of brown, the arranger reinforces expressive content.

Arranger: Mrs. W. Harrel Wilson
Photographer: Mills Steele

Plate 6   A rhythmic design accentuates the textural loveliness of Argyreia, a pearl-gray vine, with stems like velvet and new leaves like soft silver, enriched with decorative veining. In itself the vine is more shape than form but becomes form when organized in space design.

Arranger: Mrs. C. Verne Klintworth
Photographer: C. Verne Klintworth

the green of any two plants alike. The smallest and most subordinate component part of a plant is worthy of your keen attention, for each is complete within itself; Nature does not deal with incomplete parts. Disorder may prevail in Nature's complex groupings but there is nothing accidental in the masterful plan of her single units. A hand lens for close examination is a valuable companion in the adventure of looking.

Perception of visual elements may be made more acute as you walk or drive along the wayside, for the very briefness of such looking may compel you to see the essential things, to be discriminating. Study the pattern of ground swells, of streams, of drifting snow, and of the sand's "wind writing" on the beach.

When the door opens on the outside world, make conscious effort to imprint the sights on your heart and mind. If you would get the most from your adventure of looking, record your impressions in a notebook for future reference. Much of what you observe will not lead to a specific arrangement, but it will be basic in your appreciation and creativity. "May God grant you the spirit of wisdom and revelation . . . illuminating the eye of the heart," was St. Paul's prayer. So too, it is mine.

III SEEING FORM, SHAPE, AND LINE

We see an object not in isolation but in relation to things and space around it. So it is the all-embracing beauty of Nature that first draws the eye and only later do we become conscious of the details. Paul Cézanne observed that there are beneath Nature's "shimmer and sentiment, certain basic forms." All natural objects can be reduced roughly to cubes, cones, spheres, and cylinders, making form the most simple and universal factor, and the thing that grips us first.

FORM HAS THICKNESS

In form there is thickness. Its tri-dimensionality has two-dimensional shape (silhouette) and line which describes its shape. But it is the form rather than its shape or line of its shape which is most evident. This is because shadows tend to push back and highlights seem to bring forward making us aware of thickness. In Nature we cannot see separation in form and color; what we really see is color against color. An image is visible due to a contrasting background. We can realize too that while ground valleys have depth, they possess no form *substance;* they lack identifying contour of their own although they are defined in shape by neighboring forms. They, on the other hand, like every ground swell, every rock formation, every plant can be analyzed geometrically.

GEOMETRIC FORM

An apple is essentially a sphere, a pear is a combination of a small and larger sphere joined by a section of cone (Figure 1-a). Forms may be somewhat flattened as in the round shape of the crab (Figure 1-b), or elongated as in a tree trunk (Figure 1-c), a series of cylinders gradually decreasing in size as they grow out from one another, terminating in a long pointed cone. The earth itself is a combination of basic geometric forms. A low hill is roughly a segment of a sphere (Figure 2). A peaked mountain is a cone or a series of cones, upright or set at varied angles.

And within a single family—animal or vegetable—essential form remains approximately the same despite evolutionary changes.

INHERENT HARMONY

Perhaps my generalization will be misunderstood so I hasten to mention that the basic geometric shapes and forms disclosed by Nature are seldom mechanically perfect. In fact, the flaw is often as vital to an object's

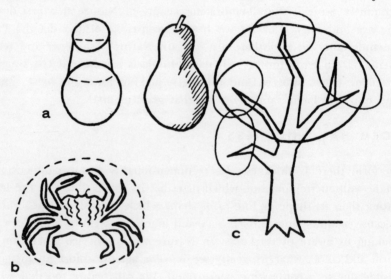

Figure 1   Objects reduced to geometric form. a—A pear is sections of a sphere connected by a section of cone; b—A crab is a somewhat flattened sphere; c—A tree trunk and branches are a combination of graduated cylinders with long pointed cones at the tips. Foliage is roughly groups of ball forms.

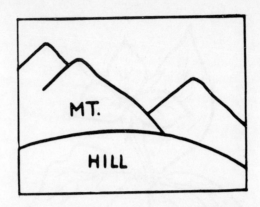

Figure 2   A peaked mountain is
a cone; a low hill a segment of
sphere.

beauty as the perfection. Adjustments are made to meet individual needs
thus preventing rigid geometric preciseness, but yet the general geometric
structures are easily recognized.

A pine tree differs from all other pines of the same variety due to a
number of causes—soil, sun, damage by elements, disease, man, or animal,
and by nearby interfering objects. But because of consistent energies
within the seed, its tree grows and remains constant in its natural form.
Like raindrops, snowflakes, waves on the beach, even leaves on a single
plant, the pines of one variety are ever, yet never, the same; there is a
synthesis in character and outer modification.

As I write, I am sitting beside a spruce, a lesson in this inherent
harmony. The fixed form or species intent is a cone developed with
branches whorled about a central upshoot. When the tree was young
a severe storm severed its top, destroying the typical pyramid. Within
a short time, however, a lateral branch began to grow upright and
gradually it replaced the main trunk to lead growth upward. With
adjustment of other branches, the tree's characteristic form was restored.
Such is the case with every species; each may develop divergencies, but
each remains true to a shaping principle, endowing the subject with
distinctive and distinguishing form characteristics.

VARIETY IN FORM UNITY

If there is any quality more plainly indicated in Nature than all others,
it is that the most appealing unity is achieved through repetition plus
variety. Indeed, such variety precludes monotony in Nature.

We agree that, aesthetically, variety is important. Why then, you may
ask, is the almost perfect pyramid of Japan's Mt. Fuji a favorite subject

Figure 3   Angular   form.   The
trillium (wake robin) is a pattern
of tri-symmetry.

in the painter's art? In the first place the near exactness of the pyramid occurs so rarely that, when it does, it is an exception to the rule and so stimulates rather than bores the eye. In addition, there is considerable variety offered within the form itself. No other shape has so much variety with so few parts as the angled triangle of the pyramid. The eye finds pleasure in a constant variation from the form's base to its tip. In a later chapter more will be said on variety; here we are concerned only with variety of form.

THE SHAPES OF FORM

Out of the straight cube and cone come the stiff and angular shapes; out of the curved sphere and cylinder come the more graceful contours. Curved shapes are Nature's favorite; she gives us comparatively few straight or angular shapes. Among the latter is the beech tree. Another is one of her most beautiful—the tri-symmetry in the triangular silhouette of the wild trillium abloom in the May woods (Figure 3). It was this plant, three-fold in all its parts, that symbolized the trinity to early herbalists. There is the lovely trumpet of the lily, hexagonal in every detail, and the magnificent angles of the Angel fish. Among Nature's

Plate 7   The presence of the designer is felt in this original composition. Strong
and interesting shapes of calla lilies, ti leaves, and one philodendron leaf pierce the
surrounding space in an angular, five-sided silhouette . . . as dramatic in its way as
a modern sculpture.

Arranger: Mrs. Ernest E. Wunderly
Photographer: Donald C. Huebler

Figure 4   a—Seahorse; b—Conch; c—Morning glory bud; d—Pitcher plant; e—Antlers.

curved shapes, those that spiral in a winding course upward are to me the most beautiful. (Figure 4). Nature seems to emphasize the rhythmic pattern of the spiral above all others. We see it in varied aspects—a true helix curve in the shell of the snail, checked to some extent in the spread of the acanthus leaf which appears as a decorative motif on the capital of Corinthian columns; it is elongated like the rhythm of a spiralled staircase in the growth pattern of pandanas, a member of the screw-pine family. I find it especially exciting in the fiddlehead fern as it uncurls in early spring. The coil of its frond is like the tip of a violin—or let us say the violin is like the fiddleheads!

Among leaves, the asymmetric begonia is unsurpassed in beauty of shape. It is distinguished by its obliqueness. The foliage is developed quite differently on each side of the center rib, tapering to a point at the tip and flaring into both right and left-hand spirals which swing forward at the stem end.

The rhythmic spiral in many seed pods is worth noting—Ixora helicteres is especially magnificent. And some of the most beautiful spiralled forms in all of Nature are seen in the animal kingdom—in the horns and antlers of quadrupeds; in the shelly architecture of ocean creatures.

Shells offer a complete and irresistible study. Some are shaped like Gothic arches, ornate with branching spines, while others are a contrast in their primitive simplicity. Some are flattish; others have deep convex and concave surfaces to delight the eye when seen from any angle. And there are shells like modern sculpture in their purity of form.

Plate 8   To the light-hearted viewer, some of the elements of early cubism are here—the building of the design architecturally, the use of natural material to stress abstract form, even the amusing possibility for turning the six to become a nine (a translation of the cubist philosophy "that pictures should look good upside-down too").

Arranger:
   Mrs. Arthur C. Sanders, Jr.
Photographer: Isadore Knox

Plate 9   Here is a statement as clear, expressive, and meaningful as a Picasso bull poster. It begins with a dynamic form, the spiral, which has all the irresistible power of the flame in nature. The brute force of the bull, the partially charred spiralled wood and the heavy ropelike roots of wild bromeliad continue to compel attention to the theme of "strength."

Arranger: Mrs. William S. Carper
Photographer: Stan Sheets

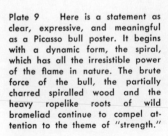

Plate 10   Free-form shapes and fern make a setting for an attenuated carving of the Madonna in this imaginative work which creates a mood similar to that of Leonardo's *Madonna of the Rocks*. How perceptively this arranger uses the rock as mountain, the wood forms as a natural shelter for the figure, and the wisp of fern to suggest sparse vegetation. Emphasis on vertical direction adds an appropriate spiritual quality to the Modigliani-like Madonna.

Arranger: Louise Hudson
Photographer: Harold Rowney

FREE-FORM

The flowing contours of weathered rock and mineral segments are natural examples of what is called *free-form*. Their non-geometric shapes have great appeal to man. Orientals have considerable respect for such fragments of rock, believing them to have a soul, a force separate from substance. Indeed, most persons will agree that free-form shapes have a vivacity not possessed by form that is characterized by a regularity in lines, angles, and curves—perhaps this is the charm free-form holds for the arranger.

SIMPLICITY

There is a lesson for the artist in the simplicity of many of Nature's forms. Skipping many possible examples, I call attention to a most familiar subject, a single stem, its foliage and bloom. Although it is not even suspected by many, simplicity reigns here. On close examination you will find that leaf color generally matches or is analogous to that of the flower stem. And while its shape may differ from that of the bloom, there is subtle transition from one to the other so that difference is scarcely discerned. Simplicity is a way to unity. This is revealed in an ordered relationship of symmetry in Nature's shapes and forms—that is, fitness in size and arrangement of parts to each other and to the whole.

SYMMETRY, STATIC AND DYNAMIC

Symmetry is of two kinds: static and dynamic. In the former there is an obvious and regular repetition of like or similar parts about a central point as in the daisy, or a basic point as in the palmate leaf of the horse chestnut, or a central axis line as in the distribution of leaflets opposite at intervals along the stem of pinnately compound foliage as the ash, or distributed alternately along the stem as on a twig of beech (Figure 5).

Dynamic symmetry is more subtle in its ordered but irregular relationship of unlike parts on opposite sides of a dividing point or line as in the abalone shell, the begonia leaf, the calla lily bloom (Figure 6).

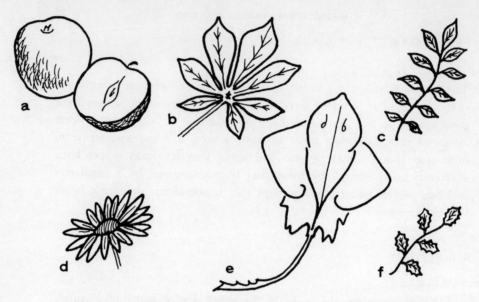

Figure 5   a—Apple: similar parts about a center; b—Horse chestnut leaf: radiation about a basic point; c—Composite leaf of ash: radiation from a central axis; d—Daisy: radiation about a center; e—Sting ray: curves within a squarish shape; f—Twig of beech: alternate distribution about a central axis.

REPETITION PLUS VARIETY

There is wide distinction in the natural world between theory and actuality, and in this the arranger can find a valuable lesson. Theoretically Nature's designs of static symmetry are easy to see and remember because they are direct. But seldom is man's eye conscious of monotonous regularity for Nature varies her presentation; there is *repetition plus variety* even in static patterns. However, the variation is so subtle that the overall effect of similarity on each side of the center axis is not destroyed. Nevertheless the difference, while scarcely discernible, does prevent monotonous uniformity. In the Canada thistle, for example,

Figure 6   Patterns of dynamic symmetry. a—Abalone shell; b—Calla lily; c—Begonia leaf showing both right and left hand spirals at stem end.

units are regular in size, shape, and color around the stem, but variety spaces them in a spiral throughout the complete flower stalk. The regularity in the arrangement of water lily petals is static symmetry, but the position of the flower on the stem gives a subtle variety to prevent monotony. In addition there generally is an imperfection, perhaps a slightly stunted petal, offset by another, so that although exactness is avoided the overall effect is one of static symmetry. You will find this condition in almost any flower, leaf, or fruit of symmetrical pattern.

FORM VARIETY TO ACCOMMODATE FUNCTION

Nature solves specific problems by using the same form over and over again, with modifications. You will find numerous examples in animal structure. The goat, the horse, the tiger, and many, many other four-legged animals follow a similar basic form, but parts are changed to fit function. To fit the pig to wallow in mud, his legs are comparatively short. A deer's legs, on the other hand, are long and strong to enable it to run swiftly from its foes.

Compared to the pig, the deer rates high as a beautiful creature, but in Nature's plan there is no beauty just for the sake of beauty; the foul-smelling skunk-cabbage is as cared for as the sweet-scented rose. Beauty is a result of cause and function. The swan, an aquatic bird, is gracefully beautiful only when he flies through the air or glides over the water's surface as he is meant to do in God's world; on land his waddle makes him appear awkward, even humorous.

SUITABILITY

All this directs attention to another of Nature's teachings—her unfailing fitness of things; in all Nature there is no law more plainly shown. It is revealed in the forms of her creatures and plants designed to suit a particular function. Among birds, for example, those that wade are elevated on long legs; those that swim have feet like paddles. In plants the cactus has swollen leaf joints or enlargements on stems where it stores water to fit the plant for survival in desert sand. And flowers, both in color and form, are designed to attract and accommodate the pollinating insect.

Figure 7   Unity in Nature by agreement of parts to a whole. a—Frog; b—Kitten;
c—Horse.

It is plain indeed that harmony results when basic laws of creation work together. In her broad plan as well as in the specific, Nature's remarkable order of harmony manifests toward simplicity. In her unified patterns everything is properly related to everything else. To profit from this observation, an arranger's composition must be appropriate to its purpose and intended expression. The arrangements in this book exemplify.

SHAPE AND FORM EXPRESSIVENESS

To break down the structures of natural things into their basic geometric shapes divulges that form fits character as well as function. To exercise penetrating vision in this manner, the sitting frog is useful as an easy assignment. View him from the front to see more easily the fitness of the parts to the whole, and resulting expressive qualities (Figure 7-a). The form is essentially conelike with the apex flattened by its squarish head. Drawn up legs are angled and attached to a cubed body within the angular frame. A dominance of angles here sets character as well as harmony and unity of pattern; the frog is quick and furtive in movement. In line with man's concept of angles, the creature has none of the soft cuddly grace of a kitten with body emphasis on curves (Figure 7-b).

These simple comparisons make expressive meaning in Nature's subjects vividly clear. To probe further, the analysis of the horse is helpful (Figure 7-c). As with the frog and kitten, view the animal from the front.

Plate 11   Nature's curves are handsomely set off by straight shape in this work marked with complete simplicity in design and execution. The container placed to expose two sides cues us to a back plane while branch direction further strengthens sculptural quality. Importance of space is a leading influence; from all sides planes are in play with it.

Arranger: Mrs. Edgar Littmann
Photographer: William Sevecke

You will see shoulders suggesting a triangle that points downward. Behind are the curved ribs suggesting a round shape. The neck, a rectangle, is topped with an inverted triangle with pointed end overlapping the neck. On top are two little triangular ears. All is supported by a large rectangle described by the front legs. This is form expressing strength in the dominance of straight shapes given greater prominence by contrasting curves.

From God's creations we can learn the language of symbolism which form communicates. Form can symbolize joy, sorrow, repose, action, and many other sensations and ideas; its messages are varied. To the psalmist, the mountains spoke of God: "The strength of the hills is His also." Indeed, broad anchorage to the ground does endow the pyramidal form of a mountain with strength and composure. Its apex reaching skyward adds dignity. When we have learned to see with the spirit as well as with the eyes, we too are attracted as though by a magnet to forms which raise our eyes far above the earth. The Lombardy poplar, for instance, never fails to impress me significantly; its up-thrust leafy arms direct my mind from earth-bound thoughts to spiritual meditation.

FUNCTION OF SPACE

As an element, space is as much an actuality as is form. It is an important factor because form cannot exist without it. A single tree or mountain pushing up into the boundless awakens us to the influence of space on form and form meaning. As margins of blank areas on the printed page rest the eye and make the print easier to read, so surrounding space makes form easy to see. And it has a quieting effect on the spirit.

When newly fallen snow covers the land, presenting a relative emptiness in the scenery, the imagination of the viewer instills details into the expanse of space. This is space functioning much as it does in a Japanese painting in which the artist deliberately leaves a large empty area. This is space that is, however, very much a part of his picture. Like the snow-blanketed scene there is room for the imagination of the viewer to enter and to move around in. Thus the artist invites the observer's participation in his work.

Space within the structure as well as surrounding it, can suggest abstract ideas and emotions. To clarify, consider the relationship of the branches and leafy masses of a tree. In the open and airy pattern of the silver birch we see a delicate elegance and refinement. With Coleridge we are quick to agree she is "the lady of the woods." We sense a freedom in trees whose leaves quiver in the air. There is no lovelier example than a poplar with its tremulous heart-shaped leaves shimmering almost continuously within a form rising high into the air. As a study in contrast, consider the oak where growth structure is compact as opposed to open in the body of the tree. This effect of solidness contributes heaviness, and soundness, as though to enable it to successfully battle wind and storm.

To understand meaningful space in design one must understand solid form as well. In days gone by arrangers thought only of form. Today they are beginning to utilize space to advantage. Space consideration is a challenge to both imagination and technical ability. Among the illustra-

Plate 12   Here is revealed space consciousness on the part of the arranger and dynamic space experience for the viewer. We see the composition as not only extending into space, but receiving space into its being. The fluidity of pattern created with space surrounded by solid balancing mass which displaces space is reminiscent of the technique in Jean Arp's sculpture.

Arranger: Mrs. Ernest E. Wunderly
Photographer: Donald C. Huebler

tions you will note examples which reveal a space consciousness on the part of the designers. Although we find arrangers have achieved worthy work in this field, a majority today still do not integrate space so that it has real meaning in their designs. For further study, *Design and Depth in Flower Arrangement** is recommended. The book fully covers the importance of space as well as the technique for handling it.

* Hearthside Press, Inc.; Cyphers.

WHAT OF LINE?

Shape has length and breadth, but line, as defined by the dictionary is "a long narrow mark without breadth, as one made by a pencil." It is without thickness. Line in Nature, as represented in stems, branches, tendrils, has at least a degree of thickness. What is more, in the growth process these lines for the most part tend to occupy more than one plane and so become a structural equivalent of form. I mean to say that line which spreads as we find it in tree branches, toward you, away from you, to the right, to the left, and down as well as up, count as orientation, for in occupying more than one plane they make us aware of volumatic space, and to the eye present an impression of shape, form and line.

In Nature's solid forms, edges are contour lines giving shape and direction to the eye. And the seeing eye becomes aware of line direction *on* shape giving design pattern on the surface of objects. A starfish, for instance, shows a radiating pattern of lines. On the seafan lines make a lacelike design. Beautiful vein tracings embellish many leaves. You will think of many examples.

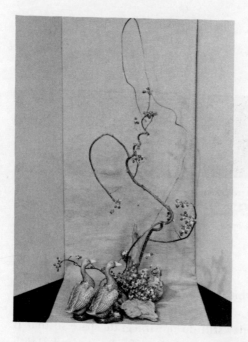

Plate 13   The calligrapher's feeling for line and spacing is carried into an arrangement of bittersweet vine. Occupying more than one plane, the woody lines effect tridimensional extension of form making the spectator aware of volumatic space. Controlling the path of the eye, note how the vine moves upward, spirals forward, then slants obliquely back into space, moving along the twig which curves to the left, and swinging down to the berried twig extending to the right of the main branch. Here the eye is directed obliquely back to the forked area. Now it moves along the other branching line, spiralling upward as it carries the eye more deeply into space. Finally the vine swings forward and returns the eye to the heavier vine structure.

Arranger: Mrs. H. Henry Staley
Photographer: William Sevecke

Plate 14 Branches of budded huckleberry create a strong experience of depth. Their crossing lines create tension, a concentration of force appropriate to the subject, *Spring Dawn.* Jack-in-the-pulpit, *Helleborus orientalis,* and pebbles complete the grouping in a lead container on a burl plaque.

Arranger: Mrs. E. Bartlett Headden
Photographer: Horace Sheldon

Plate 15   Yellow-greens of corkscrew willow *(Salix)* and Hosta variegata in a hand-made green bowl. See the appealing repetitions (veins in hosta and lines on the bowl; pattern of willow and carving in the stand). The openness of the stand relates it beautifully to the pattern of plant material, and its elevation sets off the design as nothing else could. Note the shadow which suggests mystery and therefore gives endless fascination to the eye and mind.

Arranger: Marguerite Bozarth
Photographer: C. Fanders

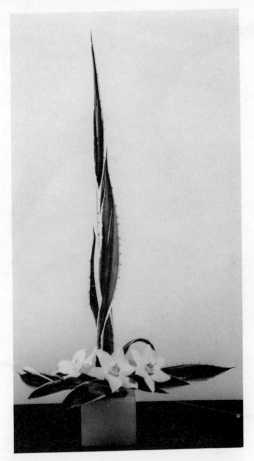

Plate 16   This is reminiscent of the force and thrust of modern skyscrapers. White-banded agave taken from the heart of the plant, unfurled and arranged in a cube of quartz, establishes a basically symmetric arrangement; the eye finds tension and repose through a balance of complementary vertical and horizontal line components. The vertical column of leaves gives a sense of depth which is increased by forward and backward swing of leaves low in the design. The vertical is emphasized not only by the subordinated horizontal line of leaves, but also by well-placed Eucharis lilies with their drawing power of whiteness to arrest the eye. at the base, thus allowing the longest possible sweep upward along a compelling perpendicular.

Arranger: Mrs. William S. Carper
Photographer: Stan Sheets

THE EXPRESSIVENESS OF LINE

Open your eyes to the expressiveness of line; impression depends largely on its direction in space. Symbolism is universal, a synthesis of all humanity's emotional experience when in the presence of certain things. Straight vertical and horizontal directions are positive, strong, and stable. For example, the perpendicular position of a tree trunk in accordance with the law of gravity expresses dignity; the dominant horizontal direction of seascapes or the open plains convey peace and calm. The vertical line is not a likeness to a tree trunk, nor the horizontal to the plain or sea: they communicate emotional far more than visual likeness.

Plate 17   In themselves the birds in the vista of infinite sky have no inherent mood; any feeling or mood is in the observer.

Photographer: Charles F. Cyphers

Plate 18   Inspired by the soaring flight of a bird, strelitzia, ti leaves, and a small pineapple are arranged in a free-form container. Except for a logic of direction, this modern composition has little natural association with flight. One feels a sense of jet propulsion due to the thrust and tension between two parallel diagonals which correspond with and are close enough to amplify each other, giving a more positive, powerful movement than if there were only one diagonal.

Arranger: Mrs. Ernest E. Wunderly
Photographer: Donald C. Huebler

Line carries rhythm as nothing else does; its force lies in the suggestion
of movement. Drifting sands in a series of flowing shellike shapes and
sometimes in crossed lines give strong lineal rhythm. The direction of a
steep incline because it deviates from the composure of the vertical and
horizontal is a line charged with activity. This is the line taken by man
when he is buffeted by strong winds, the "soaring line" of birds as they
rise or fly high into the air. In these fast-moving creatures of Nature,
all is subordinate to the movement of line, for certainly you are not aware
of feathers on the bird, nor of its form. Ripped down to essentials we get
the real force of action.

Curves have a transitional capacity, a softening influence, felt in
scalloped line of ground swells along the far horizon, or in the grace of
a meandering creek nearby. A spiral expresses generative forces. A series
of concentric curves (as when a pebble is thrown into water) because
they increase in size from a common center outward are expressive of
expansion.

In design, lines that radiate upward express growth and spontaneity.
When the eye is conscious of opposing directions spirited action is

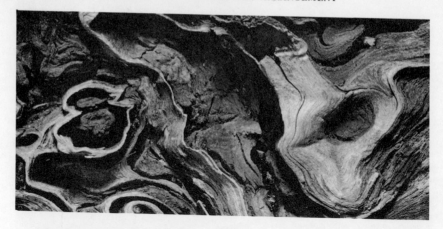

Plate 20 Calligraphy is the language of line motion which artists employ for meaning as well as beauty. Nature displays it in the grain of leather, wood, stone—in all growth rhythms. Often the motion study is like the gesture in action painting, as in a cabbage cut in half, or in this weathered wood which resembles a calligraphy of a Pollock painting. Here are interlocking spatial directions in light and dark values giving illusion of fluctuation—a continuing back and forth motion over the surface. At the same time the eye traces a flow of movement—its play, its fluidity. Tensions of stop and go produce motion dynamics in which we see one movement after another in but an instant of sight.

Photographer: Howard M. Oberlin

Plate 21 Inspiration and imagery for this interpretation—life, warmth, steadiness of *Summer's Fulfillment*—came from a piece of spiralled wood. The spiral in Plate 9 expresses strength; here it expresses generative force as well because of the way it is encircled (by white statice). Yellow daisies epitomize the steady warmth of a summer sun, thus color harmonizes with character. In the optical path upward, the spacing of beech leaves affords the eye the pleasant experience of stopping a little, then moving on. These "pause points" help balance the delicate branch pattern with the dense wood and flowers.

Arranger: Mrs. Clifford E. Cyphers
Photographer: William Sevecke

Plate 22   Inportant in this interpretation of *Summer Elegance* is the arranger's sensuous delight in the "graceful refinement of summer blossom and butterfly," and her recognition of the similarity between the palm and wing of the butterfly.

Arranger: Mrs. William E. Roberson
Photographer: Isadore Knox

characterized. Nature does not often display abruptly broken line, but when she does, as in zigzaggy flashes of lightning, in a pattern of agitated water, or in a series of very sharp mountain crags, man associates it with *restless* activity; in many, a sensation of fear is aroused. Thus we have a blending of fact and fancy.

PERSONAL FACTOR

What goes on in your mind as you look at something, rather than its characteristic line, shape, or form, may be a personal reaction. To me a spider is loathsome and arouses repulsion and fear even though I know the species to be harmless. And as I watch the gull, his arched wings almost still as the momentum of his body allows him to glide through trackless space, the idea of wild freedom is evoked. A friend relates one artist's reaction to dried cecropia foliage. She said of its fantastically curved shapes: "Even in death, I see the *struggle* for life." Association may enhance the beauty of a subject or detract from it, but one thing is sure: it certainly will affect it in some way, and the "seeing eye" is aware of this.

When through arrangement you transmit what in Nature you see with opened eyes, an alerted mind, and an awakened heart, you blend outer

Plate 23   The real and imagined merge in an arrangement influenced by the grace
and delicacy of line in Japanese etching. From a design standpoint, the positive vertical direction following the pull of gravity stabilizes this airy composition by reaffirm-
ing two sides of its rectangular frame.

Arranger: Louise Hudson
Photographer: Harold Rowney

and inner vision with fact and fancy into composition which gives substance and structure to a synthesis of thought and fact. In this way, through your art, you come to a unity with Nature for you identify yourself with her in your seeing, your thinking, your feeling.

POTENTIAL OF PLANT MATERIAL

A plant growing in Nature's garden is a different thing from one cut and used in arrangement. As it grows out-of-doors it takes characterization not alone from its individual attributes and position in space, but from its relationship with elements around it. Have you ever happened upon ferns in the cool shade of a forest retreat? If so, and you saw deeply, you noted surely, how softening their effect! But in arrangement, unless ferns are handled with great care, their patterned fronds can weaken design. And the common cattail in the open marsh stands trim and sedate like the erect and motionless heron in shallow water. As my eye sweeps the long vertical growth, it becomes the epitome of dignity and stalwart poise for all its humble origin. But in the smaller scope of an arrangement the tracery of the reedlike plant can be like an Oriental etching in idyllic grace and delicacy. The tall straight mullein as it guards pasture and roadside has classic beauty that seems an emblem of unyielding assurance, and yet in arrangement it can appear casual and flexible. In the open, plumes of pink astilbe strike a note of formal elegance; in arrangement of delicate femininity.

Plants moved from Nature into an arrangement are in a sense transformed while yet they remain the same. To list all comparisons would be an endless task and actually of little worth, for under varying environments and relationships plants, like any other of Nature's portraits, may suggest varied meanings. Do not give inflexible meaning to any given subject; let it unfold its character when and where you see it in a particular setting and situation.

I hesitate to let this incomplete reference to form, shape, and line stand, but it will have served its purpose if its briefness has shown how much more there is to be studied than we can consider unless we are face to face with the subject, the problem, and the medium.

IV ON COLOR, TEXTURE, AND LIGHT

In Nature's panorama, form is fundamental—this we know, but keep in mind that we see form only because of color against other color. Vegetation is generally thought of as Nature's most colorful element, but some inanimate objects display more variation on their surfaces. The rock of Colorado's Grand Canyon, for instance, is heralded as one of the most colorful pictures in the natural world. Color existing everywhere in Nature is a show of God's love; how drab a world without it!

Despite infinite variations in our medium arrangers are apt to think of color simply as red, orange, yellow, green, blue, and violet. As a consequence, arrangements show little appreciation for the vastness of the realm. Many floral compositions are clichés of color without the deeper meanings that a thorough understanding use of color can convey.

SEEING COLOR

Failure to take advantage of Nature's subtleties comes not so much from a lack of interest as from *inability to see* what is offered. Snow is not always white any more than the sea is always blue; both reflect sky color to be sure, but at times, the color of the earth is an influence too. And what color is the sky? If you answer "blue," please look again. Due to forces of air, cloud, frost, and sun, sky color is constantly changing; now

50

it is a clear azure or a turquoise blue, now a milky-blue, and now, gray, If the season is spring the early morning sky may even be a pale green, and the sky at night can be anything from deep blue-violet of wild grapes to a deep blue-black.

BEGIN AT THE BEGINNING

The best way to begin anything is at the beginning. Whatever else may have changed since the dawn of history, color remains the same. We know its source is light from the sun. When it passes through moisture particles in the atmosphere we see spectrum hues in the rainbow arc which forms in the sky. This colorful band seems indeed to be a bridge to heaven, as it was thought to be centuries ago.

Achromatic color (white, gray, and black) also has its source in light. It differs from chromatic color of the spectrum hues in that refraction does not break the light into component parts. Achromatic color has only lightness and darkness, no hue. An opaque object held between a table surface and a source of light will cast a shadow. As the object is moved toward the light source, the shadow lightens; it darkens as it is moved closer to the table. Thus we can register a neutral scale in progressive steps from white (no shadow) through gray to black (very dark shadow). These neutrals are distinguished by their whiteness or blackness while chromatic color is distinguished by its hue of yellowness, redness, blueness, etc.

PIGMENT THEORY

Of various systems and approaches to the study of color, the *pigment theory* is the arranger's choice, for pigment is practical and easily available for experimentation and application. The painter's pigment is the rainbow's counterpart; he strives to reproduce on his palette the bow's red, orange, yellow, green, blue, and violet. As most of us know, the most complex hues are derived from the artist's primaries yellow, red, and blue. Orange, green, and violet, made by a mixture of equal amounts of two primaries, are secondary hues. These six rainbow hues mixed in varying proportions produce additional color which science has proved is present in light although not visible to the naked eye. With chemicals, man imitates but he cannot duplicate the spectrum hues.

The secondary hues directly opposite the primaries on the color wheel are complements—that is, a primary and the opposite secondary complete each other; between them they represent the entire color spectrum. In the pigment theory these complements are red and green (the latter a mixture of yellow and blue), blue and orange (which is yellow and red), yellow and violet (which is blue and red).

We should remember that when complements are placed side by side they intensify each other and must be proportionately balanced for pleasing results. Their juxtaposition is exciting, as strong contrast always is. The complements oppose each other not only in hue, but also in character and value as well: that is, in their warmness or coolness, and in their lightness or darkness. To illustrate, orange at the warm end of the spectrum is warm, and in relation to the amount of light it reflects, is high on the value scale, while its complement, blue, at the cool end is cool and comparatively dark, therefore low on the scale of value.

DOMINANT, UNOBTRUSIVE, AND TRANSITIONAL HUE

Orange is an aggressive hue which attracts attention; it seems to move forward and tends to hold the eye so we speak of it as *dominant* hue. The same dominant quality is true of red and yellow, of very light values, and in achromatic color, of white.

Its contrast, or complement—blue—recedes, and because it tends to release rather than hold the eye, is designated as *unobtrusive* hue. So too are dark and grayed values. This attention-getting factor is the reason why arrangers use the most vivid hues nearest the eye. They reserve the receding color for the outer edges of their compositions to strengthen depth perception. Painting artists and landscape architects do likewise to suggest distance.

In the scale of hues, green lies midway between warm advancing yellow and cool receding blue, and violet lies midway between this blue and warm advancing red; they, like achromatic gray, are neutral in temperature and movement. We classify green and violet as transitional hues and use them in designing to lead the eye easily from one extreme to the other in a rhythmic sequence. The arranger can use transitional color to pull advancing and retreating color tensions into a balanced relationship.

COLOR IN PLANT MATERIAL

The chemical construction of plants determines their individual coloring and light reflectance. Few flowers and even fewer leaves approximate the purity of the spectral hues. If glanced at casually, a flower may appear to be red, but on careful analysis you will discern other hue in its makeup. In my experience, the flower nearest to spectrum red is the common poppy; other so-called red poppies show traces of orange or violet. Among nasturtiums one can find a true spectrum orange. The nearest to yellow is the dandelion; to blue, the centurea; to violet, the sweet violet (Viola odorata); and to green, grass blades and the baby leaves of an apple tree. Most other leaves show a noticeable amount of yellow or blue in their green.

Intense hues exist in plant life; as do some that are considerably grayed (varieties of orchid, tulip, and iris), and others almost completely grayed (as in mullein foliage), but most natural tones lie between a one-quarter and one-half chroma or strength. This is regardless of whether the value is dark as in the deep color of a darkening sky or light as in the exquisite pale delicacy of color in sea foam.

COLOR SCHEMES

Let us start our little excursion into the world of color interrelation we call schemes by agreeing on a basic fact: a hue is nothing by itself; it serves only in harmony or in contrast with other color. Just as in this book it is taken for granted that readers are acquainted with the meanings of hue, value, and chroma (strength, intensity), so too in the discussion of schemes it will be assumed that certain laws are understood.

Even though the pigment theory is a practical means towards understanding color, Nature rewards a perceptive eye with unparalleled guidance. We will consider first her blended schemes—gradations in values and chromas of one hue in the monochromatic, and in values, chromas of related hues (neighboring on the pigment wheel) in the analogous. Because the quality of agreement is pronounced in these related plans they are tranquil harmonies, soft, gentle, easy to live with.

MONOCHROMES

Nature is rich in simple, one-hue plans. Examine them in the overall view of land, of water, and on her smaller details of shells, fishes, birds, land animals, insects, flowers, leaves. These do not exhaust the possible sources for naturally monochromatic plans; they are intended merely as a check list. A fact to be noted is that variety is a property all have in common. You will be hard put to find in Nature a color area without some variation in value and/or intensity, if not in hue; even the petal of a flower is not without gradation from a darker value to a lighter, from a duller tone to a brighter, or both. Observe variety in mottling, spotting, or veining on petals, leaves, insects. Variety is sometimes a touch of strong contrast as the complement or near-complement in the heart of a blossom or on its pistil or stamen. In some cases the contrast is in jet-black against bright hue as on the wings of the Monarch butterfly, that beautiful creature of the sunlit hours.

ANALOGOUS PLANS

Presented in Nature perhaps more than all other color schemes, are the analogous plans which combine related hues. You can observe them everywhere. In a clear sky one can often see a good example. Much of the time its color beauty can be traced to monochromatic gradation, but at times there is variation in the hue itself which is of greater appeal; its azure tint becomes more luxuriant when it is varied with tints of green and violet-blue which the color wheel reveals as related hues. In summer's woodland we see a plan of greens, yellow-greens, and blue-greens; in autumn when foliage turns there are the bright yellows, oranges, and orange-reds to delight the eye. In winter where deciduous trees are major elements in the landscape, gray and brown dominate, but in the dry fields there is a preponderance of subtle-toned yellow, orange, and orange-red. The awe-inspiring Grand Canyon exhibits analogous plans. There is color running from dark grayed tone at the base, up through yellow-brown and varying tones of red and red-orange to grayed yellow toward the top, while in other locations the range is from gray through analogous hues in the violet family.

Like monochromatic plans, Nature's analogous harmonies are often spiced with contrast. Her balancing use of opposites is clearly evident at that season of the year when summer begins to move toward fall. Roadside asters in shadow tones of lavender and purple rest the eye that might otherwise become fatigued with the opulence of autumn brilliance. It is then too that the dark green of pine and hemlock furnish the variety of contrast to the dominantly bright related schemes of gold, scarlet, and red of birch, maple, and oak.

SCHEMES OF CONTRAST

Because the emotional appeal of related plans is, on the whole, less dramatic and easier to live with than dominantly constrasted plans, Nature is wise in stressing them, balancing them generally with just an accent of contrast. More forceful plans with an emphasis on contrasting color, however, are observed. In the reference made to the juxtaposition of complementary hues one of the schemes of contrast (direct complementary) is touched upon.

An instance is a field of orange poppies seen from certain vantage points against the blue zenith. A spring sunset often paints the western sky with a soft red-orange banded with complementary turquoise. In late summer Nature strikes an exciting chord when, among the green leaves of a sugar maple, the foliage on just one limb has turned to scarlet; it is like a banner flying high! One cannot forget the exhilarating effect of such shows, even though they are subordinated to the more quiet schemes. But for the most part Nature reserves her powerful direct complementary plans for her smaller units as green holly with red berries.

What a revelation to a colorist are the sunsets—no two alike! In addition to direct complementary schemes brushed across the sky at sundown, and the more frequent analogous, Nature is even more generous with her complementary triads of red, yellow, and blue. The combination of any triad of hues equidistant on a twelve-hue pigment color wheel is, like a pair of direct complements, a balanced plan, for it represents the entire spectrum.

The combination of unrelated hues in any triad is stimulating and in Nature, as with direct complements, is generally reserved for smaller units. What rich and gorgeous triadic coloring in plumage of many tropical birds, the macaws of Central and South America in particular.

Plate 24   In this arrangement of nasturtiums in a red-brown and brass basket on a mahogany burl, the changing patterns of light and dark, the seeming flatness of the planes, and the emphasis on linear structure, invite comparison to a Gauguin painting.

Arranger: Marguerite Bozarth
Photographer: C. Fanders

To the artist the most valuable lesson in direct complementary and triadic schemes is the attraction for, and satisfaction to, the eye. This is because these are balanced plans representing the entire spectrum which the after-image phenomenon proves are a physical need for the eye. When true complementary or even near complementary or triadic hues support the entire arrangement, they contribute to coherence. On the other hand, the very quality which draws the eye and links the separate elements may vitiate unity if the balanced plan is concentrated in just one area in a design. To insure against this, color repetition elsewhere in the arrangement will subtract from the self-importance of such combination, and the hues can then work toward unity. Never forget it is principle and circumstance not rule that determines success or failure.

LIGHT AND SHADOW

Color is influenced by the play of shadow. This may be all that is required to set a creative spirit to work. Let us examine some instances. The bluish-silver light of moonbeams transforms the outside world into highlights and opaque shadows. When a full moon dominates the sky

IA ORANA MARIA

Plate 25   *Ia Orana Maria* (Hail Mary), Paul Gauguin (oil on canvas). Gauguin's personal response to life—his ability to look into the soul of a subject—freed him from the necessity of copying Nature. His objective was to produce a symbolist art through a synthesis of the real and the imaginary. The figures here, slightly distorted, are Tahitian natives. Mary and the Child, however, appear as they might be imagined by South Sea island worshippers. His harmony is communicated to the viewer as decorative pattern—broad flat planes, colorful shapes, and decorative line influenced no doubt by Japanese prints. Of special worth to the arranger is Gauguin's fondness for patterns of light and dark values.

Courtesy of *The Metropolitan Museum of Art, New York*
Bequest of Samuel A. Lewisohn, 1951

Plate 26 Light and shadow are important aspects of this composition. They clarify the forward and backward swing of the branches, thus giving depth realization. The repetition of shapes in both the lighted and shadowed areas create rhythm without monotony.

*Arranger and Photographer:
Mrs. Paul Kincaid*

a mood of calm surrounds objects bathed in its light. In moonglow objects are mere shapes distinctly outlined, their shadows rich in mystery. As the moon wanes they become less distinct and finally merge with the sky and other objects into the darkness of night. During the sunlit day, shadows are transparent with hue visible, and shape subordinated to light and shade. Observe how light merges with the edges of objects such as distant trees and hills.

LIGHT AND SHADOW GIVE SEPARATION

Sunlight that filters through a canopy of leaves may produce a "hit and miss" pattern of light and shade that can be disruptive. Man adapts sunspot mottled with shadow in camouflaging to *destroy* form, and thus conceal objects (as the spotted coat of a fawn conceals a young deer from its stalking enemies). But in most cases, contrast in light and shadow *enhances* and *strengthens* form. Note, for example, the modeling significance of bough shadow thrown on the smooth gray bole of a beech tree.

As you see the strengthened form, notice the effect when an area of leaves catches the light and casts relative shadows on other leafy masses. Just as contrast in hue separates the planes, so too do shadow and highlight. The shadow separates these masses providing a strong contrast of bright and dull so that the areas stand in relief.

Seeing this relationship of light and dark, and bright and dull, is inevitably to reach the conclusion that in arrangement there will be sculptural relief when light-colored areas of plant material are staged against dark or dark against light, and bright against dull or dull against bright. We know it is shadow that molds the silhouetted shapes of huge rocks and mountains so that the eye sees them as three-dimensional. And it is this modeling effect of light and shadow that strengthens the dimensional pattern on windswept sand dunes, and emphasizes form when Nature folds a heavy blanket of freshly fallen snow across hill and dale. The wise designer applies such observation to arrangement.

Reference to shape and form may appear irrelevant in a chapter dealing with color, texture, and light, but the brief digression is necessary if only to declare *value* (the amount of light reflected) as important a quality of color as hue. Arrangers should not take light and shadow for granted; they should try to know it as a tool.

LIGHT TRANSFIGURES COLOR

Just as there is no form without space, so there is no color without light; as space is a quality in its own right, so too is light. Care in lighting an arrangement can make color mean more than just color. Color is not only dependent on light for its existence, but its appearance and its effect are changed by the type, quantity, and source of light under which it is seen. Many times I have noticed color seem to change as a peculiar light spreads over the countryside just before a summer storm, during it, and after it has passed. When clouds obscure the sun, the yellow-greens of foliage reflect the sky and take on a blue-green hue; the greens that spill across the shadowed fields are almost gray. When the rain comes, all greens are greatly deepened in value. Finally when the storm is spent and the sun shines again, the wet greens become strangely yellowed. Yes, light transfigures color. Sunshine, bright or pale, reflection from clear or grayed sky, from sunlit or murky clouds give enough variety even in just the greens to touch the color artist with delirium.

In arrangement never think that to get force and impact you must resort to intense color, or that the subject itself must be powerful; in Nature a hazy or an ethereal view often causes deeper emotions than one with bright-hued flowers seen under the glare of golden sunlight.

And the surface color of an object is varied with different angles to the sun (in arrangement, to the source of natural or artificial light). A tree or hillside seen from one vantage point will stand forth as dark against light, from another angle it will appear as light against dark. When things are seen in direct sunbeams, some of the surface hues (particularly of autumn foliage on trees which contain sugar in their sap) take on an almost glowing brilliancy; they are as if made luminous with an inward light. Especially does the scarlet foliage of the sugar maple glow as though it were giving back the light it had absorbed all through the summer.

At sunset, light rays from a flaming sky sometimes color earthy objects so that they take on a kind of *un*earthly beauty. At dusk when the sun has lowered but is still sending light over the horizon, it casts a purplish earth shadow in the eastern sky. It is now that all color softens. What a lesson to the arranger is this hour when Nature throws her most subtle tones over the landscape! In the strong light of day, rugged mountain peaks may seem austere and forbidding, but in the grayed tones of dusklight, they lose severity. And so it is in arrangement; color in weakened intensity (grayed tone), more than any other element, can convey a quality of gentle softness.

But this is a generalization so is highly vulnerable; Nature reminds us we should not rely completely on generalities. To observe the differences in effect between the subtle tones of the twilight hour and those of breaking dawn is an irresistble source for this fact. In the halftone lighting in both situations, color of things may be the same, but expressive quality differs greatly. At day's close the ebbing light seems passive and darkened shadows active; at day's beginning we experience just the reverse.

In the field of light on color, fascinating work is being done by experienced arrangers in shows today. Sometimes to provide a mood colored gelatine paper is attached to the source of artificial light which floods a composition. Or black light focused on an arrangement completely changes hue for unusual and dramatic effect. To experiment with light on color is stimulating and can be most rewarding.

COLOR SYMBOLISM

It is challenging for arrangers to use color for its expressive character. The trick in using it creatively is to see it subjectively. I am sure that universal symbols born of long associations with Nature—as red with fire, and yellow with the sun—are familiar to everyone. But to the sensitive individual, all color (achromatic as well as chromatic) will embody a *personal* ideal.

To me yellow, the sun color, is of a pure spiritual essence. Red, as the hue of passion, is associated with zeal, enthusiasm, optimism, power, strength, and sorrow. In the light of personal reaction it holds earthy forces to typify the total of all that is unchangeable. The symbol for orange is action. Produced through an equal mixture of yellow and red (of spirit and earthy forces), it seems to me the key color for universality. Green, the mother color of Nature, stands for youth and freshness in man's mind. I hold it in high esteem; it is the symbol of eternity like Nature herself. Through the ages blue has been the emblem of love, loyalty, and truth. As the dominant sky color, it takes on (for me) the spiritual vibration of infinity to lift me above physical limitation, and I know that love and God are one. Impersonally, violet means royalty and respect; personally it conveys compassion, for it is the union of the red of suffering and the blue of love. Is not compassion born of love and suffering?

Achromatic color is without hue, but the neutral scale has an intellectual and universal association for mankind nevertheless. Black associated with the darkness of night has long been a symbol of despair; white with the light of day, a symbol of purity; gray made from a mixture of both, of indefiniteness. But a spiritual relation reaches more deeply into meaning. Since truth and knowledge come through delving into the black depths of the unknown, black though expressive of silence is heavy with mystery and concealment; its silence is passive. White too is silent color, but a silence pregnant with something of the supernatural. It is full of possibilities like the mood of a country world hushed by a blanket of snow; while you listen to the silence, it is accented by the bark of a dog a mile or more away. Natural light is white light, the active manifestation of all life, and so white offers a symbol of revelation. And gray? It is endowed with soothing qualities which come through the combination of the active and the passive.

To yield to personal reactions such as I have done here is not whimsy; it is fidelity to self and reality by which the soul gains understanding and power. In your creative arranging remember that your soul, not the plant material, is the communicant!

COLOR AND TEXTURE CLOSELY ALLIED

We cannot speak of color without considering texture for they are so closely allied that separation is sometimes difficult. At times it is texture rather than color on which the beauty of things depend. How lovely a furrow in the earth just opened to the sun! Few who stop to think about it will deny that the aesthetic appeal of freshly ploughed ground is mainly in texture. The same is true of a lawn, else why would one slave to keep it free of weeds when their hue matches that of the grass? If Nature were to group the weeds in orderly patterns, their texture by contrast would set off the velvet beauty of the lawn. Growing helter-skelter as they do they are distracting to the eye.

Because the surfaces of grass plots and areas of stirred soil consist of minute projections and hollows, they seem to pulsate with vibrant hue. Resultant highlights and shadow lend color richness not possessed when grass and soil are seen in small amounts. In April or early May where drifts of violets purple the bank of a brook you will see a similar effect. And it is the same resulting richness of hue that holds the eye in a spread of Texas bluebonnets, or in a field of sun-ripened golden grain. In arrangement the lesson derived is of benefit when you are massing flowers of one hue; tonal variation within the area will give aesthetic appeal as rich as though several textures had been harmoniously blended. Maize Harvest, Plate 28, inspired by grain swaying in a gentle breeze reveals such effect.

Indeed, texture affects color to a great extent. Certainly man with his pigment has never approached Nature's spectacle of autumn foliage coloring; one cannot adequately describe it in just terms of red, yellow, and orange since much depends on texture. Although both the foliage of sassafras that has turned in the fall and burnished brass possess a glow that emanates from their surfaces, their golden hues differ mainly because their textures differ.

TEXTURE FOR TEXTURE'S SAKE

Just as every individual element has color, so too it has texture. In some instances (as with water and cloud), texture is the only difference. Apart from considering its effect on color, Nature should be examined for texture just for its own sake—the luster of her still waters, the matlike surface of her pastures, the coarseness of her pebbled shores.

Sometimes it is the texture of an object that is responsible for forming a definite opinion about that object. It is only the husk on a coconut that is rough, but even when its edible meat (in itself smooth to the touch) is taken from the outer shell, we think of the coconut as being rough. Sometimes texture is an entity. Water is an example, affecting change with every surface it covers.

There is much variety in texture to attract the eye—the velvet of many mosses, the spongelike texture of others; the wool of the foliage of mullein; the glasslike surface of the galax leaf; the lacquered finish of cycas. Gooseberries and many varieties of grapes are translucent; pears are waxy. It is easily possible to make further comparisons.

LIGHT AND TEXTURE

As light affects a colored surface so too it affects the texture and should not be overlooked. As I write I can raise my eyes to an amazing demonstration. A few hours ago in the dull light of a rainy morning, the pattern of vine against the brick of a neighbor's home was just that—vine against brick. Now Old Sol has shown his face and is illuminating the vine from the side, and texture as well as color is changed in appearance and character. They have come alive! The leaves cast shadow to give strong separation between them and the brick, but more exciting is the way the light reflected on their shiny surfaces makes them eye-catching in their new brightness and vivid hue. And by reason of contrast in texture, color, and intensity, the rough red brick now makes an interesting and complementary foil for the smooth green of the leaves.

TEXTURE CHARACTER

Like color, texture has expressive quality. As the character of a fabric is largely determined by the woven pattern of its threads, so is the

Plate 27   Bracket Fungus. Minute projections of surface texture catch the light and create shadow, resulting in a richness of tonal variation. In Plate 28 the maize in an inverted brass bowl, like the fungus, is in essence a monochrome with tonal variation bringing life to the one-hue plan.

Photographer: Howard M. Oberlin

Plate 28   *Maize Harvest.* The texture of the plant, like that of the fungus, is animated by catching light and casting shadow. A heavy bunchiness typical of the plant material makes it difficult to arrange artistically. It is evident that the arranger pruned judiciously to produce this aesthetically satisfying composition.

Arranger: Mrs. Forrest K. Bryan
Photographer: Blick's Studio

Plate 29　　On a charred board base, weathered wood is arranged with beige-green papyrus (like witches' brooms), chrysanthemums, and croton leaves in autumn hues, to interpret *Harvest Moon*. The strong curve of wood is a transition between the opposing diagonal of papyrus and the horizontal of the base. Note how placement of the demanding circles in the flowers gives direction, enabling the eye to move from them with ease.

Arranger: Mrs. William E. Roberson
Photographer: Isadore Knox

character of a plant determined by the texture of its leaves and flower petals.

A tree is a convincing example. The effect of its leafy pattern and bark gives texture and it varies more than color and shape. Smooth bark and small leaves thickly distributed on the monumental beech give uniform texture to this magnificent tree. Clothed in this manner the beech has rather a tender aspect without losing its stalwart character; it seems as calmly poised as Greek statuary. The smooth bark on the silver birch and a less-thick distribution of small leaves bring it an air of daintiness and an elegant grace. On the sassafras, a coarse bark and a spotted foliage texture due to comparatively large leaves of broken outline sparsely scattered on the limbs, vest the tree with an air of reckless vigor. Expressive quality springs from the size of flower petals and leaves, their shape and number, and the way they are disposed on the stem or branch as well as from the posture and motion of the plant's form discussed in Chapter III. This is so factual that the great Chinese painters of Nature represent foliage as *texture* before they add structural line to ascribe it as a plant.

In arrangement where texture is to be employed for expressiveness, sympathetic attention is required. Since the eye moves more slowly over a rough surface than it does over a smooth, when rough texture dominates in a composition the impression of poise and slowness is characterized. Glassy smoothness can convey alertness, swiftness. The important thing is to use texture related to the subject. Sometimes texture says more than either color or form. Let theme or intent be your guide.

IMAGINATIVE EXPLORATION

But the artist—and this includes you the arranger—concerned with satisfying his aesthetic appetite for color and texture through expressive qualities, should realize there is no need to literalize the elements as they are seen in Nature. Creative ideas are an offspring of imagination, one of man's most extraordinary talents. In using color and texture give free play to your imagination exaggerating or subduing the literal or the real. You're in good company when you do. Just as Picasso's horse in the Guernica mural is not a likeness of agony but a symbol of it, color and texture as well as line and form serve as symbols. Call it inventive if

Plate 30   Texture effected by surface pattern of lines. In a distinct recession of planes from front to back, overlapping shapes create an uncomplicated design in depth. Space is further expanded by the seafan's transparency making visible a shape beyond (driftwood).

Arranger: Naida Gilmore Hayes
Photographer: Helen D. Faas

Plate 31   Action conveyed in the poise of this *Discus Thrower* (copied from an early Greek sculpture), is repeated in the line of branches. Gloss on these painted branches and high polish on the figure supply smooth, shiny texture to heighten the impression. Color furthers the idea with the force of complementary contrast in grayed turquoise of the sculpture, branches, and base and orange (itself a symbol of action) in "glamellias" made by taking apart gladiolus and wiring the petals into camellia-like form.

Arranger: Mrs. Ira J. Varnedoe
Photographer: Marsh-Kornegay, Inc.

you will for invention is similar to imagination but more specific it is the ability to conceive and to satisfy a definite need.

I recall a fog-cloaked view where background and surrounding details were elminated, causing a nearby rock to stand out as a sinister shape. The low tonal value of the scene and the overall atmosphere communicated a depressing and uneasy mood. The impact of mood is always as much a part of the precept as shape and color. Here was inspiration for an arrangement of strong and powerful form with sombre gray its predominating tone, and a minimum of smooth surface (just enough for contrast). Not a matching of Nature's coloring and texture, but an exaggeration to convey a sensation within the limited content of an arrangement.

THEME, THE GUIDE

Let theme guide you always. If Nature displays a lively effect, a predominance of light color tone and smooth texture will suggest this in

Plate 32   Palmetto foliage is deliberately torn and blackened with fire not for the sake of distortion but because it relates with other elements to convey desolation, experienced by the arranger on a river mud flat in our southland. Texture of leaves, driftwood, and fungi more than any other element unify the concept. The "bird" (a root painted white) symbolizes a solitary life in a forsaken land.

Arranger: Mrs. Robert Godley
Photographer: Frank W. Martin

Plate 33   Textures run riot here
and also the feeling of color. Together, color and texture transmit
an experience of Nature, *Dawn in
a Fall Garden.* Beige-hued manzanita, reddish-orange and green
Laurestinus *(Viburnum Tinus),* light
and dark red-orange chrysanthe-
mums, handmade quail and container in deep blue with brown
overtone, and a dull brown red-
wood burl, combine in a scheme of
soft-toned related hues—color described as mellow. Textures are of
a nature which further an impression of mellowness; the chrysanthe-
mums give an effect of softly glowing highlights in a world of shadow.

Arranger: Mrs. Joe E. Wolff
Photographer: Joe E. Brown

arrangement, even though these qualities are not stressed in the actual scene. Deep tone and mat surface can well be reserved to express Nature's more serious atmosphere, and grayed hue and soft texture to convey a gentle air. Generally speaking, strong hue, dark value, and coarse texture, in combination with bold structure, carry the property of strength; weak hue, light value, smooth texture on a delicate framework increase the feeling of sprightliness and spaciousness. Luminosity is conveyed through a combination of bright hues very close in value as yellow, yellow-orange, and orange-yellow on lustrous surface. Even though white reflects light, an area of white alone is very much less luminous in effect than the area broken with touches of bright, light-reflecting yellow (yellow approaches white in the value scale).

PRINCIPLE CONTROL

The colorist interested in Nature's ways must understand the fundamental principles at work in her varied combinations. Color, texture, and light are elements of design as are line, shape, form, and space. In artistic activity, as in Nature, these are controlled through the basic principles. The role these natural laws play in organization is explored in the following chapter.

V ON NATURE'S PRINCIPLES

Mood and atmosphere describe the emotional "feel" of Nature's pictures. Color and texture identify the surface of the elements that combine to produce her views. Shape and form relate to the boundary contour of these parts. Line reduces their shapes to simplest elements. Space supports all, emphasizing line and form. Singly these properties do not satisfy aesthetically any more than they make a unified whole. A relationship which cements all into a single statement has far more meaning and significance than the identification of the component parts.

Flowers in the meadow, trees at the river's edge, mountains in the distance, the sky as background—all of these are separate elements in Nature's overall design. Yet Nature combines them so that they merge their separate identities, like the sounds and silences of music, into one total effect; the eye can see a master view as unified. For countless generations man has attempted to understand and record the basic standards by which Nature creates her patterns. The physical world is so completely governed by basic laws that we can note them here in only the briefest way. But if we learn to understand the working of those behind the various effects that attract us, Nature will be more comprehensible and a greater inspiration in arrangement.

DUALITY RESOLVED FOR UNITY

Nature produces in ones or in more than twos, never in two equally uniform features unless they are organized so that the eye accepts them as a complete unit, not as two separate parts. Flowers constructed as the violet, for example, have a duplexity of petals at the top of the bloom, but this is modified by three lower petals (Figure 8-a). Or two uniform members of a structure are combined so that to the eye it is quite evident that neither in itself is a whole; they complement each other like the horns of cattle, the wings of insects (Figure 8-b), the wings of birds, their left and right feet (Plate 17). The seedling plant is an interesting illustration. As the soil yields its life to the seed, two leaves spring from the ground but the duality is not readily recognized because the leaves curl away from each other, their directions encouraging circular eye path. As a result they appear to the eye as a single pattern (Figure 8-c). And in a short while the duality is even more resolved through a dominating central stem, and the pair has formed a group of three, a plurality (Figure 8-d).

We cannot escape the conclusion that in the relationship of things to prevent undivided attention for the eye and mind, we find *unity*. We learn that all the natural laws which we call principles of art—dominance, contrast, rhythm, balance, scale, and proportion—are unifying factors.

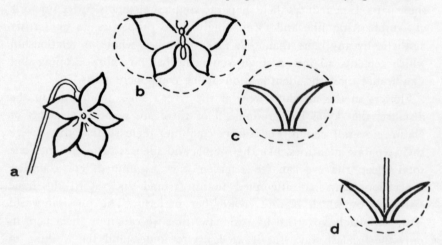

Figure 8   Duality resolved.   a—Violet; b—Butterfly; c—Seedling; d—Seedling.

Plate 34   In this interprétation, *The Strength of the Hills is His Also*, we find line and form used emotionally as well as intellectually. Composure and strength in a mountain's pyramidal shape is the design's foundation, with its apex drawing the eye upward communicating spiritual uplift. Duality in the agave leaves is resolved here, as in Nature, through mutually complementary placement.

Arranger: Mrs. Albert P. Micciche
Photographer: Albert P. Micciche

DOMINANCE

HOW DOMINANCE IS ACHIEVED

In designing, dominance may be achieved by various means—by number, by spacing and position, and through physical properties of size, shape, color, and texture. And as usual Nature guides the artist. Note how she masses small and inconspicuous bloom as babysbreath into a cluster

Plate 35   Although naturalistic in style, this spring garden is not a mere trans-position from Nature. A force and sturdiness the arranger felt in fragility of spring growth is communicated through restraint and a dominance of powerful line. Androm-eda *(Pieris japonica)* dominates through position—high placement has drawing power for the eye. A predominance of green (in leaves, moss, rocks, and container), symbol of young growth, is given added vigor with the "lift" of yellow daffodils.

Arranger: Marguerite Bozarth
Photographer: C. Fanders

Plate 36   In this concept of a windswept scene, space is modeled with everything in the composition; we react to every relationship. "Chinesey" in effect and wind-blown in direction, cattail leaves become a part of a greater harmony. The man on the bridge attracts our attention as a human figure inevitably would. In his wind-blown garment, this beautiful Chinese bronze deserves and receives plenty of space. His comparative isolation emphasizes him and makes him a dominant feature of the arrangement.

Arranger: Mrs. Raymond P. Wismer
Photographer:
    Classic Photo Studio of Westfield

Figure 9   Repetition. a—An intersecting spiralled line produces repetition of diamond-shaped pattern on the surface of a pineapple; b—Arrangement of regularly repeated scales on fish, pine cone, petals on artichoke, echeveria, etc.

a　　　　　　**b**

large enough to attract the eye. A field buttercup is so small that although it is a demanding yellow, it would escape an unsuspecting eye. To assure notice Nature spreads the little golden cups closely together to make a large area of intense color. On the other hand, she displays her large bold flowers like the bogland flags singly or in groups of just a few stalks; the blooms thus retain their identity. Were they massed in a broad continuous sweep, their tri-symmetric structure would be lost.

Repetition attracts the eye and as a means toward order and simplicity is by far the most common method for achieving dominance in a grouping of elements. A notable example of harmonious repetition is the classic pineapple, its surface "squared off" into diamond-shapes by an intersecting lineal spiral. Another is the latticed crossing of the fronds on the trunk of tall Sabal palmetto. The pine cone's repetitious scallop with an accent at the center edge of each woody scale is still another common sample. See Figure 9.

Plate 37   *Linear Construction in Space, Number 4,* by Naum Gabo. Utilizing new materials requires new approaches to sculpture. With transparent plastic and stainless steel, space is defined here by constructing rather than by carving or modeling. In viewing this completely abstract non-objective form, open volume allows the eye to see within and without simultaneously. Arrangers should note the likeness of parts to the whole—the subtle repetion of oval shapes.

Collection of the
　Whitney Museum of American Art
　New York
Gift of the Friends of the Whitney
　Museum of American Art

HARMONY THROUGH REPETITION

A strong harmonizing factor is the likeness of parts to a whole. Trees are illustrative of harmony through repetition. Or perhaps *similarity* is a better term, for the repetition is not necessarily exact. Consider the oak (Figure 10-a) and the holly (Figure 10-b) with leaf shape similar to the silhouette of the trees' green crowns. Sometimes the shape of a solid is repeated in a space area, or the reverse may be true as in Nigella pamescena where the spaces between the angular lines of the foliage repeat the shapes of the flower petals.

There is repetition in Nature's wide panorama as well as in her component parts. The eye is attracted by similar silhouettes in a group of trees and distant hills or cloud formations. Although the structures are otherwise unrelated, the eye finds pleasure in the similarity of form.

Harmony through repetition carries into color too. In Nature one hue or one group of related hues generally dominates and is responsible for a general effect or character. Working here is the principle of

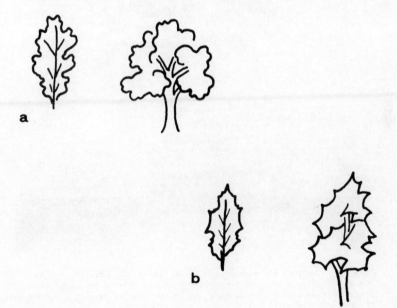

Figure 10   A similarity of shape in leaf and tree. a—Oak; b—Holly.

Plate 38   Nature's likeness of parts to the whole, has influenced this harmony. The pyramidal form is artistically satisfying because the eye so easily follows the gradual approach from base to apex; the reverse direction delights us for the sake of unity within variety.

Arranger: Mrs. Forrest K. Bryan
Photographer: Blick's Studio

dominance. A definite example is the overall delicate and lively yellow-greens in spring sweeping the countryside with crisp freshness. In summer the dominance swings to a darker green reached in the maturity of growing plants. The warm group of related hues which dominates the fall scene is displayed almost as though the color were a final flash of warmth, a stimulus to help combat the cold dominance of winter.

VARIETY IN DOMINANCE

But the lesson for us is not so much in the repetition displayed as in the differences! The very essence of Nature is change—from day to day, with the seasons, with the years. It is the variety of it all that is most valuable. On the one hand repetition attracts the eye; it is like a magnet in this respect. On the other hand the eye becomes bored with too much sameness; differences, subtle or forceful, give relief.

Plate 39   In a harmony of repetition, contrast adds to our enjoyment of this lively work. There is light and dark, dull and bright, smooth and rough, but note especially the bent stems which turn the diagonals of the feline body into a repeated motif subordinately contrasting the dominance of vertical direction.

Arranger: Mrs. Raymond Russ Stolz
Photographer: William Sevecke

CONTRAST

INTENSITY AND ENRICHMENT

One cannot deny the life enrichment contributed by opposites. Without such contrasts as day and night, wet and dry, calm and wind, winter and summer, life would lose its savor. But it is impossible to draw a definite separation between opposites; they are but parts of a whole. Without the darkness of night, for instance, we could not appreciate the light of day. We can conclude that things can gain emphasis through opposition as well as by repetition.

In single structures opposites are related through subordination with balance and unity resulting. Emerson spoke of the "rock-loving columbine" and we are reminded of the beautiful contrast of fragile flower and coarse gray stone against which Nature likes to hang her little smooth, five-petaled, flame-colored bells of the columbine. Small as the flowers are, because of hue and pattern they are the prominent feature in this setting; things always are more pronounced when combined with something less compelling to the eye. Nature frequently demonstrates emphasis through contrast, combining foliage that is smooth, sturdy, and bold in outline with patterned bloom, and vice versa. The water lily is an example. Roundness is echoed in flower and leaf, but there is contrast in the plane of the leaf pad and the sphere of the bloom. In addition the petals give pattern. Consequently the three-dimensional patterned flower, more eye catching than the simple two-dimensional leaf, is dominant. In a twining vine you can see a contrast of direction—straight upright and horizontal movement within the main pattern of curve. Because these are subordinate, curve is emphasized as characteristic of the vine. You take it from here; a list of examples is endless.

This subordinating relationship accords with that law or principle of Nature we call dominance for unless there is subordinating factor (something over which to dominate) there could be no dominance. Without dominance, disunity would result in a combination of opposing elements. Even color is combined in unequal amounts as witnessed in the Oriental poppy with its bright flower petals, black center, and grayed foliage. A significant example of dominant and subordinate relationship in contrasting textures is the acorn. A lesser amount of patterned texture

Plate 40   The intriguing balance here is so like that of a gliding bird with outspread wings. Balance is secured and aesthetic appeal enhanced through a sensitive relationship of opposing rhythms. Unity is controlled by the meeting of the branches at a center-of-interest area. Combined repetition, gradation, radiation, and transition to achieve rhythm are clearly revealed in this arrangement of peach blossoms and mahonia foliage in antique bronze on a teak stand.

Arranger: Mrs. Simeon T. Shields
Photographer: H. P. Sheldon

in its cup, by virtue of difference, enriches the nut's smooth surface and makes it dominant.

There are large scale examples of contrast and subordination too. An impression of grandeur and dignity in a landscape dominated by vertical trees is considerably strengthened when the scene is viewed in relation to a low horizon or a horizontal expanse of lake or river. Or note the value of a vertical tree seen against the circular formation of clouds; its contrast gives enrichment and emphasis to the cloudscape.

These examples show how unity is achieved through subordinated contrast, the second of three modes of organization at the artist's disposal. The character of this order exemplifying the force of contrast is vivid and exciting.

In arrangement use contrast where force is needed or intensity of interpretation is desired. If, for example, a dominance of drooping line expresses sorrow, an accenting contrast in line direction will intensify the mood; if a dominance of blue expresses coldness, an accenting subordinate contrast of warm hue will increase its chilly impression.

DEPTH ILLUSION STRENGTHENED

In Chapter IV we considered modeling effect of light and shadow, and the relief and separation when forward and receding color is combined.

We should not leave the subject of contrast without this reminder of the part it plays in the conception of third-dimensional quality.

SCALE

Scale is size relationship of units to each other and to the whole. Pleasing scale exists when units seem to relate consistently in size to the overall whole and yet appear to be their true size, neither enlarged in effect nor dwarfed. We learn from Nature that it is the fitness of things that is at the root of scale. A revelation is the size relationship between the elephant and the plants in his habitat—large plants seem properly scaled to the mammoth animal.

HARMONY OF SCALE

In art, scale refers to the size of individual units that go into the construction of a composition. To determine what sizes may be satisfactorily combined one must understand the significance of scale. There must be the harmony of a logical agreement in sizes. A hollyhock is a lesson in a pleasing consistent scale relationship of parts. Here you see the harmony of a gradual change in the size of foliage and bloom from large to small from the base of the stalk to its tip.

SCALE INFLUENCES FORM

The scaled relationship of elements has much to do with the form of any object. As usual we can learn from Nature. The shell of the nautilus famed in Oliver Wendell Holmes' poem, *The Chambered Nautilus,* owes its form to the growth of the mollusk within. A series of chambers that gradually increase in size as they circle around a point are produced in the process, and a spiralled shell results (Figue 11). In like manner a well planned arrangement grows from within, one part scaled to another, the finished design emerging as a unified whole.

Discussion of scaling by means of a gradual change or sequence in size exemplifies unity achieved with emphasis on *gradation,* the third pos-

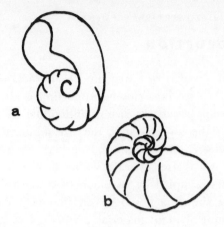

Figure 11   The chambered nautilus. a—The graceful spiralled shell of the mollusk; b—Cross section of chambered nautilus showing the proportionately graded succession of chambers by concave partitions.

sible means to order. Based on gradation there is harmony of units alike in some respects, different in others. The order differs from the two modes considered above in that organization through gradation is more subtle than that achieved when repetition plays dominant role, and simpler than order based on contrast.

Plate 41   Consider the materials here in landscape terms and see how excellent is their scale relationship—airy sky, towering trees, transitional shrubs, animal characters (possibly two self-important penguins?), a pebbled shore and lake are imagined from skunk cabbage spathes and daffodil foliage, cabbage leaves and hoods, a few stones and water in a Canton hot water plate.

Arranger: Mrs. E. Barlett Headden
Photographer: Horace Sheldon

PROPORTION

Proportion is the relationship of one part of a structure to another, and to the whole. In defining it we can see how closely proportion is allied to scale. It differs in that scale applies to the size of individual units, while proportion refers to areas the units occupy, the size adjustment between the amount of one element or one area to another. The size of a flower in relation to a leaf is a matter of scale, while the area of a plant's foliage in relation to that occupied by its bloom is a matter of proportion. In arrangement the size of a flower in relation to a container is scale; the area or amount of plant material in relation to the container is proportion.

In discussing dominance and contrast, attention was focussed on the need for inequality in amounts. Equal proportions, we concluded would present competition for the eye and prevent unity. We are already aware of Nature's delight in uneven distribution, but let us analyze her teaching of proportionate relationships more thoroughly.

DYNAMIC SYMMETRY

There is a relational matter between the length and width of a thing as a whole, and the length and width of its component parts. In design, pleasing proportion is largely a problem of judgment, and a most intangible property. We are blessed, however, with instinct which approximates the dynamic symmetry of Nature, a proportionate relationship found in numerous manifestations. Naturalists tell us this is a balanced ratio of roughly two to three (2:3), three to five (3:5), five to eight (5:8), and so on. This simply means th t Nature combines two units of one thing with three of another, or three units of one with five of another, and so on. It is widely demonstrated in the progressive growth based on a constant factor in all of Nature's spirals, in the twists of vines and tendrils, in the coil of shells, in the curves of antlers, in the shimmering webs of spiders, and in numerous other natural subjects. To be specific, examine any number of well-grown gladiolus spikes. Generally you will find five to eight open florets with three facing one way, two another, or five one way, and three another.

This mathematical progression based on natural proportions named by the ancient Greeks as the "Golden Mean," is known today as *dynamic symmetry.* Its aesthetic appeal rests in a proportion of elements that is neither too equal nor too contrasting. Flower arrangers approximate this relationship when they follow a 2:3 ratio in the familiar one and one-half times measure, a guide for determining pleasing proportion of plant material to container. On the other hand they do not hesitate to allow plant material to rise higher than the one and one-half times measure dictates; the problem is one of balance. In the final analysis, satisfying proportion of plant material to container, as well as the proportions of line, form, color, texture, and space, depend on the material itself, the arrangement's setting and the judgment of the designer. The latter develops with practice. Let us always consider the ratio only in regard to intended expression and always as an approximation, for we are dealing with art, not mathematics. Our discussion of form in Chapter III revealed that Nature has no rigid rule regulating proportion of parts to the whole. It is determined, by function—the long bill of the hummingbird enables it to drink the nectar in tubular flowers.

Because of the eye's pleasure in unequal proportions, the majority of flower show niches conform to the "Greek Oblong" determined by the Golden Mean—that is, a rectangle with sides in the relation of 2:3 or 3:5, etc. (Figure 12). This does not mean that a square frame representing a ratio of 1:1 should be avoided altogether. On the contrary, it would be most appropriate if a strong, clumsy, heavy concept is desired. Purpose is, as usual, the determining factor.

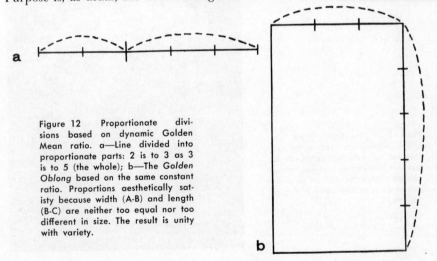

a

Figure 12 Proportionate divisions based on dynamic Golden Mean ratio. a—Line divided into proportionate parts: 2 is to 3 as 3 is to 5 (the whole); b—The *Golden Oblong* based on the same constant ratio. Proportions aesthetically satisfy because width (A-B) and length (B-C) are neither too equal nor too different in size. The result is unity with variety.

b

BALANCE

In a discussion of balance, it becomes useful to recall that color differs in hue, value, chroma, "movement," and "temperature." To be assured of satisfaction in color combinations, we must balance these differences.

LINKED WITH PROPORTION

The balancing process is closely linked with proportion. Nature, our faithful guide, avoids equality in hue, intensity, and value distribution. There are insects, for instance, of one hue marked with an accent of an opposing hue, or that are predominantly dull or dark in color with just a touch of bright hue. And often Nature backs a light pattern with dark or the reverse. In flowers her favorite balance seems to be a color difference between the petal and heart of a bloom. She fringes the bright yellow center of the oxeye daisy, for example, with rays of white which occupy a larger area. In a deep blue pansy the yellow heart is relatively very much smaller in area than the daisy's yellow but more intense, and

Plate 42   The passion-flower (Passiflora incarnata), is obviously symmetrical yet how fascinating to the eye, for Nature has supplied enough change within the pattern to dispel boredom; variety prevents eye fatigue.

Photographer: Howard M. Oberlin

Plate 43   Nature's symmetry related to a flower arrangement of pink parrot tulips, green and white hosta foliage, white double lilacs in a vase of alabaster. Light gives sparkle to the mass of pleasing textures skillfully held together not by restriction of interest centered in one area, but by several well related areas of focus. Seen simultaneously, these increase inner space, for they require the eyes' unconscious movement from one to the other. Contrast in values strengthens tri-dimensionality.

Arranger: Mrs. Howard M. Oberlin
Photographer: Howard M. Oberlin

by means of contrast with the less aggressive blue, seems even more intense than it really is. In this way it is strong enough to balance the comparatively large amount of less forceful hue of the petals. Thus we see the quantity of color is dependent upon its force on the eye; the more dominant or aggressive the hue, the less is required for balance.

The arranger needs to absorb these principles of color proportion and balance, for he works within a limited frame and cannot rely on the binding property of atmosphere to prevent discord, as Nature does in displaying her varied color areas in panoramic views of unlimited space.

SYMMETRICAL AND ASYMMETRICAL

An earlier chapter declares the daisy a pattern of static symmetry, the pansy of dynamic symmetry. Both are *balanced* relationships and at this point, worthy of further attention. Symmetry in fixed and regular plan, an equality in the distribution of mass and space about a central area, is known as symmetrical balance. In finding unity within such pattern, the eye moves from and returns to a center with certainty. The crown of a well-grown tree exemplifies symmetric poise about the central trunk. Should an outside force cause the loss of a large limb so that the tree's

Plate 44   There is a Daumier-like competence about this arranger's use of planes, line and volume. The placement of leaves breaks up the asymmetrical composition into well-defined planes, the darkness of magnolia leaves at the left balancing the superior mass of variegated dracaena leaves at the right. Manzanita branches create linear strength. Although they are on different planes they form a gentle path for the eye as it moves naturally through the structure.

Arranger: Mrs. Jesse Fort
Photographer: Warbeck Studio

potential symmetry is destroyed, an opposite limb or limbs grow beyond normal spread, and asymmetry—an equilibrium of visual forces rather than a mechanical balance—is the probable result. In such balance— that is, a balance of unequal parts around a central axis, a differing in position, proportion, size, etc. of mass and space—unity is more subtle. Its pattern is one of dynamic symmetry and as the term dynamic implies, is more lively and forceful as the eye must accommodate itself to emphatic changes within the structure. Our reaction to it is subjective— it must be felt—as opposed to objective reaction to symmetrical balance which is immediately obvious to the eye.

It would be a mistake to conclude from this that symmetric balance is lifeless, popular opinion to the contrary. The balance of everything at a structural center cannot help but be full of the energy of tension or *motion without progression*. In the mobile sphere of Lipphold's interpretation of the sun, one feels movement from within outward as in a daisy head. In fact the bronze wire construction, as you look into it, seems almost to explode in the center plane. Balance is sometimes defined as "elements in repose" but this does not mean repose in a sense of sleep; it means that an active force holds other active forces in place.

There is another distinction worthy of comment. Symmetrical balance is often referred to as *formal* but the term implies "according to established mode, regular, methodical" not formal in the sense of "refined elegance." Nature shows us many symmetrical structures but not all are found in the latter and common usage of the word. If you must have specific example, compare the richness and grace of a tropical butterfly, its lustrous wings outstretched, with the common variety of zinnia bloom characterized by a sense of ruggedness. In design, symmetrical balance may convey an impression of sanctity, dignity, refinement, and elegance but need not necessarily do so.

Keep in mind that varied symmetry supplies forces to stimulate the eye and mind. When anything is so obvious as to be thoroughly understood at first glance, it fails to hold our attention for there is nothing left to explore; the production is feeble. Take a cue from Nature and incorporate enough variety within a symmetrical composition to escape the monotonous much sameness. It is aethetically satisfying to have unsymmetric accents within symmetric structure.

LATERAL, PERPENDICULAR, AND
DEPTH STABILITY

In this matter of equilibrium, the natural need for man to relate things to his vertical axis is easily satisfied when he confronts structures laterally balanced—that is, from side to side across a vertical central axis; it is the governing law of gravity that gives man this sense of stability. But in design stability requires a perpendicular balance also, a balance from the base of the composition across its *horizontal* central axis to its tip; this is too often neglected in arrangement. Nature teaches that greater weight at the base of things gives an appearance of firm upright position.

Plate 45 An interesting study in lateral and perpendicular balance. By means of number, cattail foliage dominates the composition but the three lily pads are important shapes. Isolated in an area of space they are "quiet spots" to rest the eye, and as a focus of contrast with the massed area of cattails and birds to the left, hold the whole together in balance and complete unity.

Arranger: Mrs. Howard M. Oberlin
Photographer: Howard M. Oberlin

It is the rare exception when plant material is not thickened where it grows from the soil. And have you noticed that in a bloom spike, the largest form and deepest color is generally toward the base? The foxglove (Digitalis) is example. A tree buttresses itself against the ground with a spread of roots to carry the height and breadth of its branches with perfect poise. In the animal realm, legs stretch out at the feet for stabilizing support; look at the hoofs of horses, the paws of dogs, the feet of elephants.

Traditional technique in arranging follows Nature in this respect with the largest forms and deepest hues, and/or a thickening low in the design. In artistic work, care must be exercised in the placement of the weighty materials toward the bottom of a design. Guard against the prevailing tendency among arrangers to group material here in a compact area producing heavy, unpleasing bulkiness. It is possible that this may even make the lower half of the plan seem heavier than the top half thus preventing perpendicular balance. Assemble an arrangement's ingredients so that space moves under the plant material to avoid a heavy pressed down anchorage to the container or to the plaque on which plant material might be combined without a container. With this technique the eye has no trouble moving on into the pattern of the design.

Plate 46   Technique and talent work as one to produce this exquisite *Line Arrangement in Dry Material* in tones of brown. The hand-thrown tan and brown container is dull textured; the base, a tan and brown soapstone slab. Harmonious relationship exists between the design made of plants (sansevieria, fruitless mulberry, and oleander seed pods) and that incised on the container. Note how space moves under, around, and through the plant material. When, as here, the viewer is able to look through the composition, there is a tendency to relate the back to the front, making a physical third dimension a reality not an illusion.

Arranger: Beth Beutler
Photographer: Harold Rowney

Plate 47   The solid of displaced space in fungus, croton leaves, and chrysanthe-mums balances the space designed with solid (dried grapevine) defining an open area. Space moves under the bottom mass, preventing an unpleasantly bulky, pressed-down anchorage to the base. At the center of interest, forms are of dominant shape and color but not in static focus; their progressive unfolding and evolving, are dy-namic, and therefore in keeping with the fluidity of the whole.

Arranger: Mrs. William E. Roberson
Photographer: Isadore Knox

THREE-DIMENSIONAL CONCEPTION

All principles are applicable in organizing planes from left to right, from bottom to top, and from front to rear. It is the latter, the relation to depth, the dimension that goes away from you, that more often is neglected in arranging. To enable us to feel depth more acutely, study

Plate 48   Picturesque view from *Skyline Drive, Virginia.* All design stems from Nature and a scene offers many suggestions. Ideas to note: Form is visible due to contrast of light and dark; space is emphasized by overlapping planes; distance is evident through perceptual gradient, paling color, diminishing detail; curves have softening influence (the effect of scalloped lines of ground swells along the far horizon); transition has unifying character (trees are transition from sky to earth).

Photographer: Howard M. Oberlin

Plate 49   The near-far quality or perspective has special appeal in this arrangement of primroses and Korean barberry. The designer created a strong impression of depth by forcing the eye to travel from a foreground through a driftwood "frame" to dwell upon the rear plane (much as you would look through the structure of the large tree in the natural scene). Configuration of the barberry brings the eye back to the front plane again. Texture here is more basic than the recognition of the branches themselves. Each berry and leaf is smooth but in close proximity they visually break up the area into textural pattern. Thus in plastic expression visual and touch qualities are kneaded together as texture.

Arranger: Mrs. Louis H. Amer
Photographer: Lewis Henderson

Plate 50   In the lively manner of a Miro, the arranger produces an amusing composition in which we can feel the strong sense of relationship so striking in Miro's Surrealism. Space and depth are conceived here by directing the eye inward by means of the brass giraffe (work of Simon Kops) placed diagonally in contradiction to the picture plane. The triangular base of wood is scorched to bring out the beautiful motion pattern of its grain, and to give coloration to harmonize with the reddish-brown of the fascinating dried branch so right in line and character.

Arranger: Mrs. William E. Roberson
Photographer: Isadore Knox

first the broad view in Nature. A basic discipline for you is to train your eye to see distance through the effect of perceptual gradient—mountains getting smaller and less distinct in outline as you move away from them, with detail diminishing, and color paling to grayish tone.

But distance or depth of space is not solely dependent on natural perspective. In a distant view note how objects appear to overlap, strengthening a consciousness of space and distance. Oriental art has long been inspired by such observation, the artist using overlapping planes to suggest space and distance. As a matter of fact, artists of the modern school use this device rather than linear perspective to define space.

For unity, a three-dimensional composition requires balance from the front to the rear. This is _depth balance_ of which artists designing a space-art structure must be keenly aware. The arranger achieves it through careful relationship of front, middle, and rear planes. The eye must be able to move easily from the front to the back and return to the front plane again. Color, texture, directional shape, and spacing all play a part. You will find it helpful to study the arrangement illustrations to determine how depth balance is accomplished; analysis will be found in a number of captions. See especially Plates 50 and 51.

RHYTHM

UNITY THROUGH RHYTHM

In this matter of depth balance we become aware of the importance of rhythm, a movement dependent on interconnected areas of accent and pause. Logic and rightness determine scale and proportion; interest and balance govern contrast; rhythm ties the whole together. When we are exposed to natural beauty, it is Nature's rhythms that are largely responsible for our stimulation; consciously or unconsciously we are affected. Watch the rhythmic movement of fish in an aquarium, or through a glass-bottom boat see the swing of seaweeds in response to water currents. This will help you understand the influence of rhythm on one's mind for one feels a sense of unity in the presence of such persistent rhythm. Wise

Plate 51   In plastic organization the root is not something which grew underground, but a series of balancing lines, and the anthuriums are not red spathes with yellow flower spikes, but shapes of color and texture to carry the eye to the rear, increasing spatial illusion (developed mainly through overlapping planes). Shiny surfaces, repeated in the black glass of the harmonizing, free-form base, are pleasing contrast to the dullness of stone and line material. In any unity, vitality depends on the strength of forces which are in balance, and on the way the forces exert their influences. The viewer's unconscious attempt to seek balance finds it here in a rhythm of line opposed to solid, static form in the head of feather rock.

Arranger: Mrs. Ira J. Varnedoe
Photographer: Marsh-Kornegay, Inc.

is the arranger who takes stock of natural rhythms, for in design it is rhythm above all else that draws the viewer's attention and invites his closer examination.

RHYTHM IS THE BIG THING

Rhythm is basic to existence; in fact, all Nature moves to it. Rhythm is evident in the repetitious phenomenon of bird migration, in the cycle of the blade and ear of corn, in the flow of sap, in the metric march of seasons, in the rotation of low and high tides, in the lapping of ocean waves, in the tempo of day and night. One could go on enumerating natural examples of *sequences* of measured and repeated factors with which we associate *movement*.

Rhythm is also basic to art; without it there could be no masterful painting, no delightful music, and no soul-stirring poetry. An arrange-

Plate 52   In *Dance, Ballerina, Dance*, radiating lines express a lively and spontaneous rhythm. Relating the calligraphy of branch lines to the choreography of ballet, the arranger has created a sensuous composition to delight our eye. The branches in themselves do not resemble the attenuated figure, but the arranger's vision and use makes us see a similarity. The branches painted black (to match the black figurine) are de-naturalized, thus giving them abstract quality. Roses are grayish-pink; foliage is magenta-hued dracaena. Phonograph records rhythmically stacked make a fitting base.

Arranger: Mrs. Jack Welch
Photographer: Al Alleman

Plate 53   Inspired by summer's cooling rain this monochrome in green fulfills the desire for something "visually cooling for a living room table." The "raindrops" are especially worth noting; their transparency, appropriately unsolid, prevents forceful shapes from appearing heavy. Further description on page 119.

Arranger: Mrs. William S. Carper
Photographer: Col. T. W. Cooke

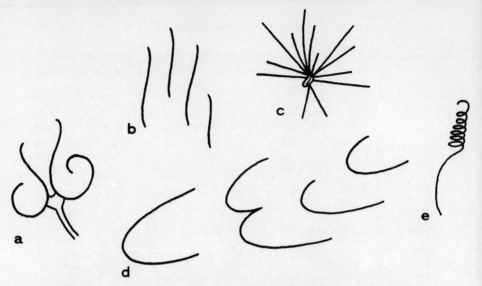

Figure 13   All of Nature's elements have an essential rhythm. a—Open spiralled rhythm of leaves on a carnation stem; b—Rhythm of grass blades; c—Radiating rhythm of thistledown; d—Curved rhythm of clouds; e—Tightly spiralled rhythm of passion flower tendril.

ment without the appeal of rhythm would be of little interest. If we are alert to Nature's teaching we will remember that in artistic expression just two repeated notes will not establish rhythm; three or more are required to supply movement of *succession,* a flow of rhythm.

Although Nature supplies plants with groups of leaves, petals, bracts, in even numbers (bracts of a dogwood tree for example, are, four in number grouped around a center of inconspicuous flowers), she builds the majority of her growing plants in threes as in the trillium, or on a multiple of three as in the lily, or in fives or a multiple of five. Roses, for instance, can be counted by fives. Because of the tendency of the eye to divide a group composed of even numbers into separate groupings, odd numbers appear more rhythmic than even. Artists construct designs on units of three, five, seven, or nine more often than on two, four, six, or eight. Beyond nine the eye is not conscious of number.

INDIVIDUAL AND DISTINCTIVE RHYTHMS

In spite of Nature's fondness for repeated design there are differences in the distinctive rhythms among her various elements. Rhythm in growing grass blades differs from that in trees and from that in cloud formations (Figure 13). The gull lifts and closes his wings as it swirls in broad sweeps and then lazily glides to complete a circular path. The little goldfinch moves in direct, scalloplike flight, the snowbunting wings its way in tilting swoops, the heron floats as though it were lighter than air. A deer leaps with long bounding curves; an elephant walks with slow swaying motion. Figure 14 diagrams examples of rhythms in natural scenery. In its representation of movement at varying tempo, what an inspiration to the alert arranger is all natural rhythm.

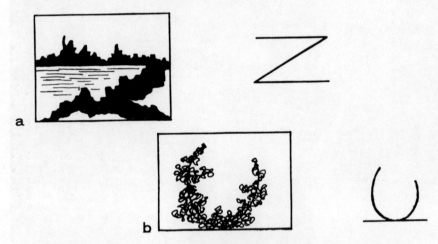

Figure 14   Natural scenic rhythm. Subject matter in these studies is purposely made indistinguishable so as to better see essential rhythm. a—Rhythm of the Z; b—Rhythm of the U.

VARIETY IN RHYTHM

Repetition is basic to rhythm but for aesthetic pleasure repetition is not fixed and mechanical. The free dynamic rhythm we find in growing things reveals a valued variety. Remember that evenly distributed units and intervals, identical in shape, size, and position, assure a sense of constancy. However, never forget that repetition without variety can be as sleep-producing as the forward and backward motion of a cradle, or the tick, tick, tick, tick of a clock. Through instinct both ear and eye respond to rhythmic repetition but both quickly lose interest when the repetition is not varied to some degree; repetition plus variety reaches above instinct to aesthetic heights. Even within such repetitious pattern as in the design of a six-cornered symmetric snowflake, there are differences. When this marvel of Nature is magnified one sees clearly the

Plate 54   In *Mutation of Sea Life*, described on page 119, note that the base is an important feature, not subordinated as in traditional work.

Arranger: Mrs. Raymond P. Wismer
Photographer: Classic Photo Studio of Westfield

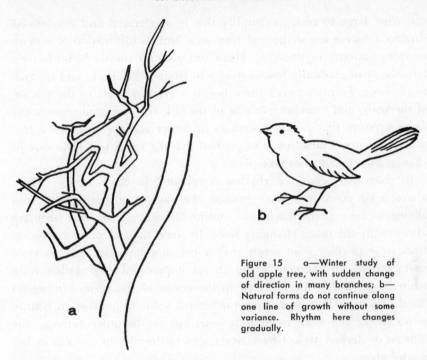

Figure 15   a—Winter study of old apple tree, with sudden change of direction in many branches; b—Natural forms do not continue along one line of growth without some variance. Rhythm here changes gradually.

varied line and shape within the symmetrical repeat supplying some dynamic quality. This is true also of the rhythm in the patterned wings of a butterfly. In trees, especially old trees, characteristic branching shows change in direction, a dominant major rhythm enhanced by a subordinate minor rhythm (Figure 15-a). Many other examples lie afield for a perceiving eye, for no form in Nature continues along one line of growth without some variance in direction. Change may be slight or it may be forceful, but it always lends a degree of movement, a characteristic which Nature's objects have within their normal forms. You will see this applied in the illustrations of this book.

GRADATION IS VARIED RHYTHM

A favorable means toward varied rhythm practiced by Nature (and the artist!) is *gradation* which was commented on above. This is a growth of line, shape, color, or tone expressed in an orderly and gradual change. The hollyhock referred to in the discussion of scale, and the simple pattern of fish scales progressively changing in size from small to large and from large to small, exemplify this in accelerated and decelerated rhythm. Observe the shape and form of a bird as illustration of a more complex pattern (Figure 15-b). Head and body are similar forms but see how the head gradually lessens in size in front to the beak, and in back to the neck. From the neck there begins a gradual swell to the middle of the body, and from here lessens to the tail. It is this same movement by progression that carries a stem to its flower and the trunk of a tree to its branches. Transition is so gradual that the eye is scarcely aware of *change,* but change does take place.

In color the beauty of rhythm is revealed in those sunsets where atmospheric conditions have broken the rays of a setting sun into analogous color plans. Each hue continually changes in tone, blending always with the other changing hues. In some natural plans transition from color to color is so subtle that it becomes apparent only on close examination. An example is the almost imperceptible gradation from white to greenish-white to green in the center of the white bindweed's floral trumpets. The change from one tonal value to another in Nature seems to become more rapid as it nears one or the other extreme, the lightest or darkest area. I have never seen uniformity in the size of her graded areas.

The importance of gradation in color rhythm is amplified by John Ruskin: "Gradation is to color," he said, "what curvature is to line." Just as the arranger can utilize curved line to carry the eye from one part of a design into another and into the space which supports his design, so too he can use color gradation from dark to light or light to dark, bright to dull or dull to bright. The influence this treatment has on depth is revealed in Nature's aerial perspective, with objects paling and graying as you move away from them.

OPPOSITION, A FORCEFUL CHANGE

In rhythm as in balance there is value in variety of contrast. Vines, you will recall, reveal counter rhythms as they twine and intertwine, moving up and down, forward and backward, in and out. Trees are illustrative too. In the union of trunk and limbs a dogwood shows an exceptionally forceful contrast in rhythms of growth. The tree grows dominantly upright, but its branches grow from the trunk forward, backward, and sideward in a pronounced horizontal sweep. In arrangement a number of plates display skillful handling of opposing rhythms, but I call your attention especially to Plate 40.

RHYTHM AFFECTED BY OUTER FORCES

Then there is rhythmic movement which results from an outside force of natural elements. The winds especially are responsible for varied and fascinating rhythms. The rhythm of tall grasses is upward, tapering to a point like an arrow, but when played against by wind, the grasses are freed to assume curved rhythm. Wind movement differs greatly among trees and yields a variety of impressions. The radial symmetry of palm is enlivened into dynamic rhythm when the fronds respond to a lashing breeze; they swish in large curves whipping backward and forward with a lively flourish. The vase-shaped elm tosses its leafy green plumes up and down in a restless fanning. Lombardy poplar lowers its head as though in worship. Reluctant to be earth-bound, the flutterlike rhythm of autumn's falling leaves awakens one's poetic sensibility as the eye is swayed by leaves moving first sideward in one direction, then in another, at times spiralling upward before finally and gently coming to rest on the ground.

PRINCIPLES INTERLOCK

These terms which have been holding our thoughts—repetition, radiation, gradation, and transition—are modes of rhythm, but so too they are embodied in other principles as well; we have touched upon them in varying connections. In an attempt to separate the inseparable it becomes obvious that it is impossible to isolate any one of Nature's laws; all work together toward a unified combination of likes and unlikes, with *unity within variety,* a result.

Of the numerous natural objects that reveal principle interlocking, the century plant (Agave) is worth special notice. Foliage dominates the succulent plant form. It is dominantly gray-green and of smooth texture, but variety is supplied in yellow or white margins and in the contrast of mahogany-red spines. Leaf blades five to six feet long, and six to eight inches wide, are repeated units radiating from a basal rosette. These are relatively spaced around a vertical central axis giving the plant graceful three-dimensional balance. In converging low on the form, the leaves supply sufficient "weightiness" to equalize the force of height, and stability is satisfied. Progressive increase in size of space intervals between the leaves provides rhythmic transition from solidity in the body mass to surrounding and supporting space, with the tapered tips of the graded leaves moving the eye easily from blade to space around it.

UNITY WITHIN VARIETY, THE GOAL

Artistic arrangements frequently follow this familiar growth pattern of progressive change to result in unity of composition. Many examples in this book achieve a three-dimensional distribution of mass and space balanced around a single source of radiation within the construction of the floral plan. This is traditional practice, but it is only one technique in assembling plant materials. Plates illustrate other possibilities. If these examples are not enough to prove the worth of such technique in arrangement, inspect, please, the diagrams in Figure 16. You will find unity, for the placement of the units in space, their directions and balanced tensions, supply an easy eye path through the design. The various parts are seen simultaneously, and the whole without the traditional center of interest is taken in at a glance as it were—a design with conflicts resolved so that there is no eye competition between parts.

To appreciate arrangements without the traditional skeleton convergence, one must free himself from conventional limitations. You will meet this problem in greater detail in the chapter on *Nature and the Abstract Arrangement.*

A MATTER OF TIMING

Space is not only a foil to emphasize line and form as discussed earlier but it can control eye passage throughout the design. As to the importance of space relationships in vision, we have an example in the dome of a star-studded sky. Our interest is not held for long unless the eye can quickly find some reasonable connection among the stars—a connection such as is shown on an astronomic chart. In the summer sky, for instance, a pattern defining the large dipper is implied by lines traced from one star to another, with the small dipper above it. Without some such space interval timing to control the eye when one looks up into a starlit sky, attention is quickly lost for interest is scattered without order.

Figure 16   Silhouette patterns of abstract arrangements.
a—Bird in flight with long tapering leaves in cup pin holder extended on steel rod. The lower leaf is looped at the base so the stem end can be pushed through a slit in the leaf and attached to the needles.
b—This design originated in observing the great blue heron standing like a statue in shallow water. It was composed of foliage and bittersweet vine from which all leaves have been removed.
c—Mahogany-red poinciana pods in a black container give unified distribution through direction and tension in this abstraction. It was inspired by overlapping planes of rounded mountains seen from a distance—evocative of strength and austerity.
d—The idea of the generous sweep of a shore line became the essence of this abstraction. Peeled wistaria painted black in an ebony bowl.
e—Although some recognizable effect can be seen here, the design is an overall impression of a scene without literal translation. Material is foliage and driftwood.
f—Form given to feeling of a bird in flight with foliage and hydrangea flower in cup pin holder extended on a steel rod.

Figure 17   Unity through *implied* line with movement from mountain to cloud to land at lower right to land and tree at left. Eye moves along vertical of trees to mountain, then the cycle is repeated. The eye may begin anywhere and move in any direction—from left to right accords with the way we read.

Nature is often helpful in her guidance of space interval timing which so greatly influences visual oneness. There are many scenes which offer no unifying continuous line to attract and carry the eye along a directed path—line such as might be provided by a winding brook, by the outline of trees against the sky, or perhaps by the flowing edging of distant hills. The eye, however, is often led by implied or subjective line (Figure 17). Just as in the star patterns, this unifying line is felt rather than actually seen; the eye is drawn from one area of interest to another so that it is the observer's imagination that completes a line. In the open landscape the interest areas may be clusters of bloom, trees that dot the meadow, even a cloud formation—any area with sufficient force to attract the eye for momentary pause. Note how your eye is urged along by direction and spacing of the various units, allowing the eye to move on along a directed path. This is accomplished not only through direction and repetition (the eye is so constructed that it spontaneously seeks repeated units), but through tension areas in the forms with a balance of rest and motion thus established. It is a physical fact that the eye requires rest areas in *any* looking. Refer to Chapter III. In considering space interval we are reminded that space is meaningful —a vital, integral element in design, not something left to chance.

TO SUM UP

To summarize all the many details we have been discussing, we have but to look at a growing plant. It is rewarding to look up into a tree and to read its essay on design. We read of harmonic symmetry, of varied

Plate 55   Directional lines—actual as well as implied—create continuity of vision which is so important to unity. The eye moves easily in a path from the lower anthurium, to legs, body and trunk of the elephant, and then by implied line to the anthurium spathe in the middle plane. From here the eye passes to the large low leaf on the right. Actual line directs it upward and toward the left-hand grouping. Implied line carries the eye from the tip of the high anthurium spadix onward to the tip of bamboo stems. These stem lines bring the eye back to the lower leaf. Thus a cycle is completed, and the eye begins again its unconscious but rhythmic experience.

Arranger: Mrs. Eric H. Feasey
Photographer: Roche

subtleties, of ordered unity in shape, line, form, and of relation of its parts to the whole. It is an exquisitely related unit with the scale of its leaves adapted to the shape and size of the parent tree. On a skeleton of radiating branches which determine the tree's form is carried a dominance of leafy mass distributed according to the law of dynamic symmetry. Each part reflects a quality of art in its adaptation to function. Branch, twig, and trunk do not continuously lessen as they grow to their tapered tips as one might think on casual scrutiny, but maintain a constant thickness until a point of subdivision is reached, and on in rhythmic progressive stages achieving beautifully balanced proportions. The bole at the base slopes to the ground gripping it with an easy transition from vertical direction to the horizontal spread of the land. In a large specimen roots spread out along the ground's surface, presenting a sense of support and balance without a sinking-into-the-earth look. In a foliaged tree repetition in shape and in hue of leaves results in a dominance of mass and color. Even though Nature repeats a particular species over and over again in its natural habitat, for each she plans a balance of contrast in upward and outward rhythms, in straight and curved. In this way subtle differences prevent monotony in sameness.

VI SAY IT WITH ARRANGEMENT

YOU MAKE THE DIFFERENCE

How does one interpret Nature's portraits in arrangement? What is seen as the potential of organization with plant material? Observation is only a beginning; we must learn to read her works in terms of personal relationship. A scene or object is before one. But what, exactly, is the content for interpreting in creative arrangement? Something seen in Nature furnishes fact and surface attribute, a basis for interpretive theme, but properly the content or holding power is *personal* response to what is visible to the eye. The arranger does not use plant material to express a mountain. He uses it to transmit the mountain's impact on him, what it does to or for him, what it causes him to think or feel, what it says to him about itself.

Oscar Wilde has told us that art begins where Nature leaves off. Aristotle wrote that "art completes what Nature cannot bring to a finish." Delacroix, in his *Journal,* said that Nature serves the artist only as a dictionary and that naturalism is the antithesis of art. Something of natural quality can of course be included in interpretive expression, for actuality as well as intellect and imagination are components of art as they are of life. But a creative work dealing as it does with illusions which touch reality of *spirit* is, before all else, a personal product of the artist. Never is it a copy or imitation of any subject.

108

Plate 56   It is exciting to observe the imagination of the arranger at work in *Star of the East,*
a blue and gold Christmas arrangement of dried plant material. Cutting away the fleshy substance from
a fresh castor-bean leaf, leaving
only the skeleton of radiating ribs
attached to the leafstalk, she created a form to fit her message.
When gilded and covered with glitter dust, it became the star rising
above gilded leaves and hydrangea blooms—the latter only lightly
gilded so their blues related the
design to a sky-blue textured fabric
background. The container, a brass
cake plate, toned in with the gilded
material; its roundness symbolized
the world.

Arranger: Mrs. Henry Bircher
Photographer: Howard M. Oberlin

To be imitative requires only technical skill. The result says nothing
of the subject's meaning or character nor anything personal, only: "This
looks as nearly like the physical identity of the subject as my medium
will permit." Greatness resides not in the subject but in the way the
artist *feels* about that subject, the meaning it holds for him. Roger Fry
in *Vision and Design* reports a child's definition of drawing as "I think,
then I draw a line around my think." In the same way the creative
arranger *feels,* and with plant material gives visible form to that feeling
whether his inspiration is a visible thing or one which comes out of
himself as sorrow, gaiety, and such, or simply compositional design.

In Nature a cypress tree in outward appearance may look like any
other cypress tree, but differ greatly from a cypress brushed on canvas
by Cézanne. The difference is the artist's personal reaction reflected in
his painted tree—the actual and the observed *plus* the artist. Cézanne,
the father of modern art, did not become a great artist until he learned to
"realize his sensations" when he painted. His emotions were far more
important than his subject. In the eighteenth century two individuals

within a short time of each other painted portraits of the same model, a Mrs. Siddons. Finished pictures were as different as the artists themselves. Reynolds, an intellectual gentleman, stressed the serious character of the actress, while gay, agile Gainsborough emphasized her affable charm. Indeed, personal expression is the first blossom of creative art.

Consider your reaction to a severe storm. Perhaps terror is aroused by its destructive forces, or the sensation you experience may be the excitement of conflict. What different people feel about the same subject is a tremendous variable, for one's feeling is a personal thing influenced by his life's experiences. For the creative artist who attempts subjective interpretation of the storm, the content to be expressed is not a visual likeness but a significance in the spiritual province, a feeling materialized and made visible to others, an emotional intercourse if you will. Bowie in *On the Laws of Japanese Painting* speaks of this as *felt nature*. The creative artist is not content with mere representation, a "faithful appearance"; he is concerned with an expression of the human spirit. What he *senses* in the storm is of greater drive than what he *sees* in it. His desire, we might say, is to communicate an experience through a visual counterpart of a psychological impression or effect of the storm, not the storm as his eyes see it. This is seeing inwardly; it is *conception* rather than *perception*.

TRUTH BUT NOT FACTUAL THINGS

The artist does not attempt to improve on Nature nor to change it; he is still concerned with *truths,* but not with factual things. In an artistic interpretation of a subject, detachment from the visual image does not imply a lack of reality, for a purely personal translation is expressive of an inner reality, an essential character which is very real indeed. To express inner reality the artist looks for the meaning hidden within Nature and within himself. Because form is given to feeling, the truths are of the spirit rather than of the intellect, but are truths nonetheless.

DESIRABLE IMPACT IS IMPORTANT

And so it is in creative interpretative arrangement. The important ingredient revealed in your work is *you.* And when this happens your work will be alive. Sad or gay in spirit, it will be alive! Again, the *personal experience* in seeing something is of greater consequence than the thing you may be looking at; you must sense the spirit or character. To do so you must exercise that inner eye, that penetrating vision discussed in an early chapter. Creativity is akin to original concept in the sense that one sees qualities of a subject in a way that differs from another's way of seeing. This difference may well lead to a desirable impact in communicating your intent, an impact that draws the viewer again and again, for this is what true art does. The arranger supplies the sense stimulus which reaches the viewer and stirs a consequent response within him.

This impact is vital and not to be confused with an impact of "shock value" that is bizarre or grotesque. The latter repels and is something to be avoided in arrangement. Such impact will draw the viewer, but his attention will be momentary. As a result he will not participate in the designer's work and thus communication is defeated. In arrangement beauty is a first requirement.

INSPIRATIONAL STAGE

Nature-inspired arrangement is simplified by deciding first what picturesque ingredients of a given subject move you to think or feel strongly about it. One of the essentials of Nature—form, line, color, texture, light, space—may predominate but all are present to some degree. Selectivity is an invaluable determinant in the creative aspect of interpretation. Ask yourself: What does this mean to me? Is it aesthetic pleasure in line, in shape, in color? Is it a powerful form, or a play of light on a form? Is it unique rhythmic movement? An intriguing mood? Whatever is the fascination for you, it will be insight that selects essential character, and rejects the superfluous. The need to eliminate non-essentials from a subject to aid clarification in communication cannot be over-emphasized. Learn to extract only what is pertinent to your theme and to discard what is not. In other words, *learn to see in the abstract.*

To this end concentrate on leading lines and masses of light and dark in your subject. It is helpful to squint your eyes until color and detail are excluded. What remains is essential, rewarding you with suggestion rather than depiction. Then completely close your eyes. That which you recall will be the relevant facets. The image will be a synthesis rather than a representation.

PRIVILEGE OF DEPARTURE

To depart from the literal—from the merely photographic image, the artist may exaggerate as well as eliminate to achieve a desired end. At base there is nothing new in distortion to enforce meaning. Among the Old Masters, El Greco comes to mind; among the Moderns, Van Gogh. Both freed their subjects from imitation through distortion. But from the one concepts held no individual feeling, while from the other personality emerged. In El Greco's religious subjects, for instance, one senses a mythical quality but one that is the same for all Christians, not personal response to religious mysteries. On the other hand, Van Gogh conveys strong intimate reaction to his subjects. *The Starry Night,* for instance, suggests an exciting explosive character, certainly a personal feeling for it is totally different from peace and stillness which is the general association of the starry night.

When the arranger distorts he does so to make his work truer to the impression the subject has made on him, to strengthen personal feeling.

Plate 57   By distorting natural shapes and colors, Van Gogh expressed personal reaction to his subject. A lesson for arrangers is that one's personality determines how we see or feel, and so can differ among individuals. Van Gogh, so uncontrollably passionate, saw the starry night as violent motion. The swirling shape of cypress in the foreground is echoed in the swishing twirling rhythm of the Milky Way; distinguishable stars are like little explosions of light over a sleeping village.

The Starry Night by Vincent Van Gogh
Courtesy of The Museum of Modern Art, New York

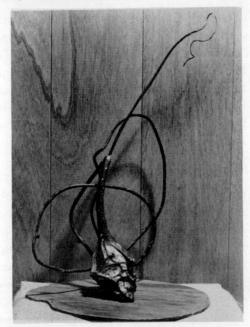

Plate 58   A green and brown gourd and honeysuckle dried and painted green on a shaded green base shaped as a palette compose a highly imaginative composition titled *Lion Tamer—From a Modern Palette*. This arranger, feeling the direction and force of the twining vine, uses it not as honeysuckle but as a pattern of interwoven lines. With the plastic forces of lines and shapes, the viewer models space as he looks into the composition, through and around it, and between the parts. The technique in this design of solid and space can be likened to *Woman Standing With Guitar* by the sculptor Lipchitz.

Arranger: Mrs. Albert P. Micciche
Photographer: Albert P. Micciche

It is your right to use the false to heighten desired effect, but beware! Such practice can be a virtue, but also it can be as habit-forming as morphine and then it may spell corruption.

TO GAIN THE ULTIMATE

Once you are satisfied that your subject has yielded its significance, decide the approach you will pursue. Will it be dramatic design? Will your work appeal to the serious-minded? Or tickle the funny-bone? Emotions embody many variables; the arranger need not work always within a serious vein. A humorous concept can be refreshing. I have in mind an amusing hanging composition, inspired by Paul Klee's *Migrating Fish*, a fanciful painting. It was constructed of foliage (well hardened by underwater submersion) and thin wire. In the spirit of fun I selected leaves of different shapes, cutting bits from a few, twisting others here and there to give them fish-shape impressions. By taping wire the length of each little "fish" they could be curved—some forward, some backward. With attention to rhythmic spacing from side to side and from the front plane to the rear, I suspended the leaves on wire from the ceiling of a large window enclosure. My "sea" of "fish" animated by actual motion in the shifting air currents, was a "fun arrangement" which gave many hours of pleasure.

Whatever your plan determine what order of organization will best fit it. Will it be a simple design accomplished with an emphasis on repetition? Or will you decide on a harmony with emphasis on gradation? Or will the drama of emphasis on contrast better suit your interpretation? Whatever your approach, whatever your plan of order, remember that technique is but a *means to the end,* not the end in itself.

Technique is, of course, important, but keep in mind that *the ultimate end in creative art is to communicate* rather than to display technical skill. An art form must hold creation for both the artist and appreciative audience—creation for the artist through conveying his concept, for the viewer through evoking a worthy response within him. Compositional relationships will unite all into a statement expressing that which inspired you to make the arrangement; pleasing relationships of movement, rest, direction, volume, void—all Nature's influence—inspired by Nature's principles of unified beauty to stimulate the spectator's approval.

You are dealing with impressions and feelings, so composition must become a matter of feeling too. You can never be sure that "this is the only way," for in art as in mathematics, the fact that two plus two equals four is no more correct than that five minus one equals four.

Your own life is responsible for your placing emphasis on certain things; composition is just another freedom pointing a way in life. Freedom does not mean that the artist is free to ignore the laws of Nature for these are common to all great art and must be respected for unity. It does mean, however, that he can choose to ignore man-made rules thereby allowing him to work within the latitude of principles with unlimited flexibility and freedom.

UNIFIED DESIGN

The creative artist is working with impressions and emotions which are true and real but to reach the onlooker he must adapt a unified form. A lack of oneness is the greatest detriment to expressiveness and good design. To achieve an impression of completeness in the arrangement, there will be some repetition to attract the eye, some variety to hold its interest (but unity not variety must predominate), perhaps some contrast to afford visual impact, an equilibrium that is asymmetrical more often than symmetrical (though not necessarily so), a rhythm to give vitality. It is through rhythm more than any other principle that you infuse your work with dynamic force.

PRACTICAL APPLICATION

So much for theory. I must move into a more specific field.

A landmark in my looking experience, and one that continually has fed my inspiration, I shall call *Cypress Silhouettes*. I am not so much interested in describing it physically as in describing what to me was the "sense of within." I stood at the edge of a Florida lake which afforded an outlook on space. A setting sun toned the sky and water to a soft rosy glow striking a note of serenity to this quiet scene. From the gentle ripple of the water just beyond, bald cypress trees rose in lonely grandeur and hushed tranquility. Against the setting sun, their silhouettes leaped into prominence as tall gray shapes. They seemed like a devout audience, even as I, listening and watching in the presence of some sustaining Power. A bird, a tiny shape in the distance coursing the low horizon, caught my eye; in isolation and in motion it exerted great force bringing a sense of aliveness to the static beauty. At the same time the distant figure, through contrast with the nearness of the trees, pointed up the vastness and emptiness of the open waterscape, and space became an important essential in the scene.

Intellectually, the aspiring and tapering growth of the trees jutting from the water of the lake designated a dominant rhythm in relation to the horizontal horizon and sweep of the water. Emotionally, this roused a sense of intense power and strength which was greatly intensified by lack of transitional curves. A straight fringe of shore gave a quality of stability or anchored certainty to the impression.

To recognize the stand of trees as bald cypress was not important— that they held an association of dignity, however, was. The impression of dignity came in part through their height although it did not depend alone on the tallness of those trees. The contrast of their dominant vertical direction with the subordinated low horizon line was a greater influence. They seemed to push against this stabilizing anchor adding to the sense of vigor and strength. Then too, the trees were fairly near me as I stood on the shore, and trees rising to a height of twenty feet near by are more impressive than distant trees that rise to one-hundred feet or more.

Here were mixed responses. In the interest of unified arrangement it is advisable to interpret only one of several aspects of a subject, but variation in arrangement can come from differing ways of seeing a subject, as well as from dissimilar subject matter. It is the spirit of dignity in tree and space which I would choose as a theme.
my fancy would narrow as a choice of theme.

I saw this waterscape as a scene that made its own frame, but one that was non-restricting with the whole arc of the sky above, the great sweep of water below, distant vegetation at the sides, and depth with shore line and projecting trees near, and horizon far. But Nature is not an arrangement, and to interpret it I would be faced with the problem of relating the natural scene to art. An arrangement, though, can be an impression of Nature depicted within a definite area of reference, so I can cut into the scene with four arbitrary limits. An arrangement is a self-contained unit which determines space and, therefore, proportions with the composition's structural border. When you begin to compose you at once determine such a frame, a frame which exercises a powerful influence on space and on the area of solids as well, lending emphasis to a direction that in the design accords with it.

We know it is the arranger's privilege to adapt what he sees and feels to benefit his intended expression: Nature's panorama is only the starting point. So even though the scene, *Cypress Silhouettes,* was viewed as it spread horizontally before me, I planned to accentuate dignity by fitting the arrangement into a vertical composition; this would reinforce upright character. I would emphasize tallness by composing within a rectangle some three times as high as wide. (Any vertical object looks taller in a narrow vertical plane for there is room only for upward eye direction.) This would give a sense of vertical expansion, a free stretch upward such as the trees enjoyed in their actual setting.

My intention would be transplanted into a self-contained arrangement with repetition in the linear structure establishing a dominant vertical rhythm. Far removed from the visual likeness of the trees, the vertical in this interpretation becomes a visual counterpart of dignity—a sensuous symbol, not intellectual. But aware that repetition in itself does not create beauty, I would consider pleasing varied space relation between repeated verticals. Variety in the outline and height of these structural lines will stimulate interest just as dissimilar outline and height added attractiveness to the natural scene which inspired me. This does not imply imitation of the natural scene, but rather a duplication of Nature's process or methods.

Nothing exists by and for itself so the vertical direction must become just a *part* of the unity rather than the whole. With this in mind I would introduce low in this design the force of complete contrast in a minor horizontal rhythm. Not only would this be a stablizing factor, but by virtue of difference and position would enforce upright character. In addition it would supply an essence of difference to prevent the boredom of unvaried repetition, and at the same time would give visual impact, for contrast tends to draw the eye.

Colorwise I would employ plant materials to provide a contrast of dark grayed hue with warm, light rosy tones as perceived in the view itself. I cannot say which thrilled me more—the pattern of dark and light or the contrast of dullness in the trees with the glistening sheen of the water. My decision would be to emphasize the latter so to accord I would combine dull and shiny textures.

ON THE TECHNICAL SIDE

I would arrange the opposing areas of direction, tone, and texture so that the vertical, and the darkest and dullest material, would dominate and be directly in front of smoother texture, slightly brighter hue, and lighter value. I would plan a movement from dark to light to increase a sense of space. All would be arranged to carry the eye by implied line to the rear of the composition where a figure of a bird with open wings and in good scale relationship would be positioned low in the design, but raised from the floor plane. I would select a light gray-blue figure to effect distance as aerial perspective in Nature suggests. And an open void between plant material and the bird would be more dramatic than a filled area. And what is more, this would by power of suggestion engender a dynamic sense of space. I would depend on the placement and the directional pose of the bird to direct the eye's return from distance to the arrangement plane.

It might be well to stress that not just any bird figure would do; it must relate to its space and to the area of plant material in some way.

I should select it with size, color, and shape in mind, not arbitrarily for the purpose of establishing a sense of space.

Like any good arrangement my completed composition will have several areas of greater and lesser attraction for the eye, but interest would not be climaxed at a spot known as the focal area such as is found in a plan where all structural lines meet at a given point. Instead, in construction the various attention-getting areas would be balanced through repetition, spacing, and direction to draw the eye by implied line. In other words, directional shapes, tensions, and space intervals would produce that line of continuity, that all-embracing contour that unites a design in a oneness of structure.

Parenthetically let me say that it is the arranger working in the freedom of modern designing that awakens his audience to the fact that there are valid means to attain unity in design other than the traditional way of centering interest at one main focal area.

SUITABILITY IN PLANT MATERIAL

And what is the best plant material for this interpretation? I would prefer to contribute only the raw material of concept, and ask *you* to make the choice. To do so would enrich understanding through personal implications and connotations of meaning. However, in the interest of practical application the following would to me be intensification of an experience. Elements would be simple: For upright placements, two to three tall, thick, smooth rose-red stalks of the castor-oil plant would be sufficient. I would remove side-shoots and foliage except at the tips of one or two stalks. A cone-shaped cluster or two of spiny dark red castorbean pods directly in front and low would supply textural and tonal contrasts. The horizontal plane would be gray driftwood. For color interest I would treat this with maroon-red water paint, brushed on and immediately rubbed off with a soft cloth to leave only traces of red in crevices of the wood.

Strengthening any theme consists largely in making one's own selection. Then it is truly the designer saying something of his own special feeling about the subject interpreted. The important thing is to be enthusiastic in your search for the just-right plant material to interpret any subject. Without enthusiasm you cannot see, think, or feel strongly about a thing.

Look and ask questions with your eyes, mind, and spirit, and then make your choice.

A MOOD FOR COMPARISON

We are mindful that in organic Nature, environment may change potential symmetry into asymmetry. In my mind's eye is a picturesque windswept tree, its root footed in a small pocket of soil among dry rocks, and its trunk obliquely overhanging a barren cleft. And I see not alone the beauty of the scene—I see its potential organization into an art form. For comparison with the above subject, this offers a totally different inspiration and problem. The moving force of my eye along the trunk bent by gale and storm blast, and through the lines of storm-swept branches sets up a corresponding movement within me. Seeing inwardly, it is a persevering resistance to force that becomes the association to be conveyed through arrangement. How might this be projected so that it becomes substantially visible? As in all subjective expression, personal concept is more important than the subject, so to me, the psychological impression of persevering resistance carries more impact than the windswept tree. A simple well anchored design in a strong diagonal linear rhythm will express this inner reality, the "felt nature" of this wild view, and if the observer understands my intent the work will speak definitely to him of my impulse.

Summer Coolness, and *Mutation of Sea Life,* Plates 53 and 54 illustrate ideas transformed by the penetrating eye and the understanding and imaginative mind into materialized ideas with something more powerful than whimsy. Suggestive power in *Summer Coolness* is immense: inverted wine bottles suggest raindrops; papyrus, cool green parasols; a lump of glass, ice. The rhythmic beat of the ocean in *Mutation of Sea Life* is intimated through the design and pattern of the base. Fan-shaped skeletonized cactus pads in the arranger's concept, "assisted the 'big one' to swim." All elements are assembled to produce creation, not to simulate actuality.

FACT AND EMOTION

All this stress on inspiration drawn from spirit or characterization of a subject does not mean that motivation cannot come from a surface reality, a factual thing. A possible case would be a washed and dripping scene viewed when the sun first appears after a long and heavy rainfall. The thing that attracts is not merely the fact that ground and vegetation are wet, but the *wetness* itself—translucent and luminous in the sunlight. It is the *effect* of the subject's factual substance on your mind and imagination that counts and serves to inspire creative arrangement.

Wetness is a surface quality and so texture is an important factor in the arrangement. To reach the spectator with this intent there is justification in spraying plant material with a transparent plastic, or brushing it lightly with oil or wax to produce a shine inspired by the appearance of the water-covered vegetation. This artificial treatment is not an attempt to imitate or represent a surface likeness of the subject but to convey wetness as an abstraction drawn from the subject, a rain-washed scenic view. Motivation is definitely subjective—that is, personal as opposed to impersonal or objective.

A FRAGMENT MAY INSPIRE

Heightened perception may lead towards selecting just a fragment of a whole as a theme rather than the overall picture. For example, let us suppose in a scene of several trees just one is chosen as your subject. You must first decide what you want to say about it. Is it the idea of elegance that is important to you? Or is a liveliness, a sturdiness, or a vigor more significant? Or perhaps an impression stirred by the thrust of the tree's branches as they buffet a gusting breeze creating a mobile yet stable form is worthy of interpretation?

My inspiration will be the felt nature of wind movement in long dancing curves of tree limbs set free in a cool breeze—so fresh, so joyous they seem. That the tree is a weeping willow at stream-side does not enter my thinking; the inherent grace it bends upon the water is of greater significance. For the sublimation of the grace of willow branches in the wind so the beholder can understand this character-impact, there would be advantage in developing an arrangement form of lyrical line and shape. We can define arrangement form as any whole produced by organized relationship of its parts. Specific types of relationship give rise to certain effects. And so, a defining form can be an important factor in rendering expressiveness as well as unity in this imagined problem.

We considered form expressiveness in an earlier chapter, but we must return to it here. One of the most effective to reveal lyrical grace, and unfortunately, one of the most maltreated, describes a reverse curve shape defined by the beauty and grace of Nature's "line of elegance." This is the elongated S. Although its use can be traced to ancient art and we find it was consistently employed by Michelangelo and Rubens, we know it today as the *Hogarthian curve*. This is due to an eighteenth century emphasis by William Hogarth, an English artist and author, on the beauty of this gently curving line so plentiful in Nature.

I would rely on this familiar form not because of its popularity among arrangers, but because its delicate curves speak to me of "grace" and thereby help to convey what is in my mind better than any other.

But we must not lose sight of the truth that while forms can be described in references to definite expressive property, expression is not limited to any made-to-order mold. Like all other elements of design, form is simply instance; by itself it may be entirely meaningless for everything is relevant. Form defined by line and shape may not of itself be sufficiently powerful to excite emotion. Much depends on relationship and integration. You may put well-chosen materials together with varied surfaces, planes, projections, and hollows molding the combination into a prescribed direction, but expressively it will not mean much until the elements of shape, line, mass, space, color, and light are well integrated and carefully related to each other, to the design as a whole, and to the space which supports it. So it is apparent that it is not the chosen form alone that builds your interpretation, but the organization of all that goes into it; all elements of the finished composition become a part of each other as well as of the whole.

An attempt to make my point would be a curved and flowing silhouetted structure with stability and a feeling of grace (my intention) developed by introducing minor straight or angular areas to contrast a dominance on long curving line. Contrast, let us remember, by virtue of difference supplies a balancing factor, provides relief from monotonous repetition, and emphasizes intended character. I would relate these different shapes to carry the eye to a center of interest area, a technique more familiar than the unifying distribution employed in the suggested interpretation of *Cypress Silhouettes*. Each part would be arranged so that it flows or grows into the other, the whole unfolding as restfully and smoothly from this interest center as a tree from its trunk spreads its

Plate 59   Ducks on the water demonstrate the optical power of repetition, the repeated units becoming a picture through direction and interval. These shapes, because they correspond with and amplify each other as they follow in succession, create an optical sense of movement—a path or line of continuity.

Photographer: Charles F. Cyphers

Plate 60   Note the strong affinity between form and line. The curves of Jerusalem oak restate those of the embryo palm egret. The bird image offers pleasure less for its naturalistic suggestion than for its function as design, a part of a greater harmony. All elements seem to relate well. An oval silhouette controls the design, but it is subtle, for the viewer's imagination must complete the shape through implied line. In spite of movement within the composition, the boundary endows the whole with the oval's symbolism of ease and contentment.

Arranger: Mrs. Robert Godley
Photographer: Frank W. Martin

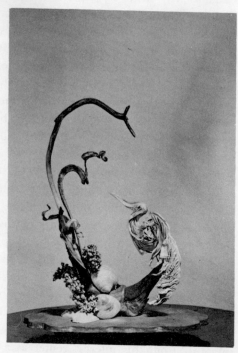

Plate 61   Plastic design by the use of a succession of repeated shapes is applied
here. The white circular shapes (chrysanthemums) are balanced into a tension area of
eye attraction. (Their demanding color and shape is not overpowering.) Repetition, a
fundamental condition of harmony too, occurs in curves and angles of the figure
subtly echoed in those of the bare branch entwined with trumpet vine. Background
fabric is pale pink textured silk.

Arranger: Mrs. F. Palmer Hart
Photographer: William Sevecke

branches into space. Not neglecting the importance of rest in the eye movement, pause points would give the eye the experience of resting a bit, then moving on. Moving the eye too quickly along the curve is a general tendency in arrangements constructed on the Hogarth curve. Color would present a rhythmic flow from warm to cool. Thus it would be the relationship of line and shape within the design aided by a delicate blending of cool color as well as the form of the total composition that would arouse the beholder to appreciate what I felt.

SUBTLETY DESIRED

Above all, we should work for subtlety in definition of shape and form as we find it in Nature herself. Avoid preciseness in geometric boundaries in the component parts of your design. This matter should have special attention when circular masses are included within the pattern of the structure. A circle is a demanding shape. Attracting the eye, its lack of directional projection retains the eye. Because of this eye-drawing and holding power, an area of circular shapes within an arrangement is apt to demand undue attention. An aid in preventing this is to position the circles so that the area will have directional projection to move the eye from it with ease. Another means for preventing round shapes in an arrangement from becoming too overpowering is to carefully space them so that their balanced tensions provide a directional path from one to the other.

If the defining boundary of the arrangement as a whole is a geometric silhouette, there is need of subtle treatment. Such is supplied when the viewer's imagination is called upon to complete the shape through implied line. Or an accent of form or mass at some point along the outline to render it incomplete will give a subtle version.

If expressive quality attached to geometric shape and form is counted on, be assured that even though the arrangement form is not exact in geometric contour, an impression is enough to convey the meaning and to give the unity basic to geometric structure. But keep in mind that it is never imperative to compose within a preconceived geometric boundary; free-form silhouette developed through original design concept is many times more effective and appealing. (The next chapter will provide analysis of free-form.)

ABSTRACTION IMPERATIVE

These descriptive examples reveal that when character replaces visual likeness of a subject, the means by which it is accomplished is abstraction at least to some degree. Abstraction is the withdrawal from—the separation of—the essential from the unessential, the distilling of essence. From commentary thus far we must conclude that abstracting, complete or partial, is important in subjective interpretation, and therefore vital to creative expression.

VII NATURE
AND THE ABSTRACT ARRANGEMENT

Like artists in all fields, the arranger has learned to see in a new way. Moving on from literal representation as in the naturalistic design, the modern arranger is expressing the inner reality or characterization of a theme in interpretive arrangement. Philosophically, to abstract means to separate from closely associated perceptions or ideas. In flower arrangement the vision which takes its subject from the visible world, strips it of physical or surface detail to arrive at the essence, the abstract *force* of the image, affirms the art as a living one for it reveals change.

VISUAL SYMBOL OF THE CENTURY

Abstract technique is often referred to as the "new trend" although abstract quality in art is as old as art itself. Ancient primitive sculptures, for example, have abstract quality due to an austere simplicity and distortion inherent in the work. The effect of abstraction, however, was accidental, a result of concept. The ancients achieved it unconsciously and as part of their culture; they exaggerated certain features of the human figure and eliminated others for the sake of symbolism. In portraying gods, for instance, faces were grotesquely distorted to instil fear in the beholder, or the abdomen of a mother deity emphasized to symbolize fertility. Today abstract effect results from concept too, but there is a *deliberate* direction toward exploring and developing the technique for its own sake. Because of this conscious effort toward abstraction it is generally considered to be a product of the modern artists.

A deliberate approach to abstractionism (the theory and practice of abstraction) came into being through both negative and positive channels. Negatively it developed as a break with tradition and positively as a determination to express in art medium, new aesthetic experiences which came with new opportunities and situations in the twentieth century. Seeing things in new relationships—like a skyscraper or airplane view of a city—has been strong influence in seeing new shape and form patterns and this in turn, has led to personal compositional styles. Mondrian's architectural painting, *Composition in Brown and Gray,* for instance, is a pattern of interrelated geometric squares and rectangles which has no visual likeness to any actual object or view, but it may well have been inspired by an awareness of shape and form relationship seen as one looks down on as common a thing as a parking lot!

TWO GENERAL DIRECTIONS

In surveying the broad field of abstract art we need some classification. For convenience we can divide the practice of abstraction into two general directions which places emphasis on the *purpose* of the artist rather than on the significance of the work. Composition without expressive content— like the Mondrian described above—that is, without the portrayal of a definite theme-subject represents one of two general kinds. Actually, the artist has no subject beyond the composition itself—he works in the field of pure design relationships. The organization of space with shapes, color, and texture becomes his subject; his work conveys nothing but order, with appeal and interest dependent on the artist's imagination. Then there is the second general type—composition inspired by a definite theme-subject. Even in this expressive work, the subject is not always discernible to the viewer. In Brancusi's famous fish sculpture, for instance, one does not recognize a fish, but the form holds inherent traits—its grace and movement.

Plate 62   *The Fish* by Constantin Brancusi. We do not see a picture likeness of a fish in this simple polished form, but the essence of its shape and graceful movement. Seeing in this way is feeling, for it comes from within. If the appeal of this abstracted fish is to exist for the viewer, he himself must enter into the spirit of the sculpture. Plate 19, *Bird in Flight*, also illustrates the artist's ability to abstract an idea—that is, to distill the spirit of the subject without actual representation.

Courtesy of Museum of Fine Arts, Boston

Various terms are used to designate work involving these two distinct differences. The most popular, and those used in this text, are *non-objectivism* for work with no subject other than composition itself, and *abstract-expressionism* which refers to expressive art—composition portraying a definite theme-subject chosen by the artist.

Seeing from new points of view represents a revolution of the eye, a new way of seeing, so this book attempts to stress awareness, to comment seriously on abstract theory and practice. There is no better way to intensify deep seeing than by abstracting.

BREAK WITH TRADITION

Design inspired by new ways of seeing is definitely a break with tradition for until recently, the conventional function of the artist had been to depict naturalistically; today he moves from the material into the spiritual, the emotional realm. The main line of development in new and original concepts stems logically from the late nineteenth century French Impressionist movement which tried to capture on canvas a momentary aspect of a subject. Monet and Renoir conveyed impressions of objects such as a haystack or a church perhaps, in a variety of atmospheric conditions—in rain, in fog, in sunlight. In seeing in a new manner, Degas carried the eye's revolution a long way. As a favorite subject he strove to snatch off-stage moments of the ballerina, the casual gesture or expression —the dancer yawning, scratching her back, tying her slipper lace.

However, we must not think of the break with conventional practice as an isolated happening for the Impressionist painters themselves were influenced by their heritage from the past—each especially influenced by some specific art form or style.

And even before Impressionism there were a few prophets of the change to come. Among them was the sculptor, Rodin. It is right to think of him as forecasting modern interests, for in a society which expected visual likeness depicted, he dared to omit natural detail in an attempt to stress characterization over surface quality. While Rodin's efforts and those of the Impressionist painters still had material likeness, they revealed concern with spiritual quality; moments of sight for the artists had become moments of insight.

From Impressionism on, it seems that painters reacted vehemently against the status quo, freeing all obligation to imitate or idealize Nature. With imagination set loose Cézanne distorted Nature to satisfy his pictorial compositions; Van Gogh distorted to strengthen expressive intent. Braque and Picasso broke up natural forms to reassemble them with the idea of expressing three-dimensional form in two dimensions. Finally, early in the twentieth century, Kandinsky sought to show painting as something complete in inself rather than as a picture showing any reference to the natural world. With his *Improvisation* he severed art from any link to a visual likeness of subject matter. The first totally abstract composition is spontaneous and intuitive work which *is* something instead of *about* something.

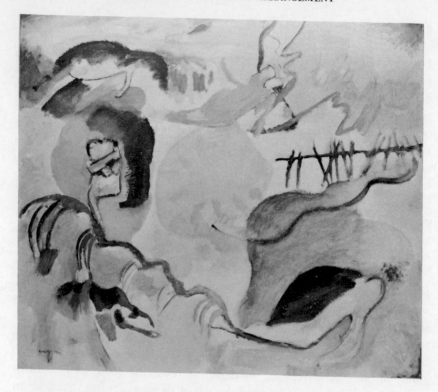

Plate 63   *Improvisation No. 27* by Wassily Kandinsky (oil on canvas). Kandinsky theorized that by eliminating all natural representation, organic abstractions with relationships pleasurable to the eye as music is to the ear would fully express the inner man. The attitude required for a viewer's appreciation depends not on recognizable objects (if present they are completely incidental or accidental), but on the stimulation of psychological response to the relationship of elements. When I identify myself with the picture in this manner—by entering it with freedom of mind and eye—I feel, even in the black and white reproduction, a strong, restless mood in the combination of heavy and soft free-form shapes, and thick and thin line, some straight, others bending, sliding, wiggling, winding. What do you experience?

Courtesy of The Metropolitan Museum of Art, New York
The Alfred Stieglitz Collection, 1949

NEW VISTAS IN SCULPTURE

The influence working in the minds of European painters affected sculpture too. Rodin, for instance, began to work in semi-abstract style. His *Crouching Woman* clearly displays the force of distortion.

Among impressionist painter-sculptors, the work of Degas and Matisse show continual experiments in space and movement. Movement expressed

Plate 64   The arranger, seeing in a new way, introduces us to materials disguised and exploited in this decorative-abstract (non-objective) composition. Small cup-holders, painted black and inconspicuously wired to a black wrought iron spiral, hold lacy arborvitae in contrast to bold "flowers" made by looping fresh corn husks. For *texture interest*, velvet lines the niche; its hue is deep yellow-green.

Arranger: Mrs. Thomas H. Ward
Photographer: Horizon Studios

through the position of a figure's body, the extension of arms and limbs into space invite the observer to move himself around the sculpture to see it from different points of view, in itself revolutionary feat. As a Cubist, Picasso interested himself in the relationship of mass and space, sculpting man's head as geometric shape, and later with complete abstraction, conveying the *essence* of structure, mass, and solidity.

We cannot ignore the sculpting of Brancusi as an important contribution to freedom from sentimental naturalism. His well known *Bird in Space* abstracts an idea rather than tells an obvious story. The long, smooth, polished shaft reveals his search for not only the essence of natural form, but the essence of sculpture itself.

Today, there is probably no sculptor who has traveled more experimental corridors of abstraction than Lipchitz; he has bequeathed to the modern world numerous sculptures which vary stylistically and conceptually. The scope of his work makes clear that abstract art is *discovery* as well as *search*. In looking for new and attractive adjustments, the artist discovers a particular answer to a particular problem. This em-

Plate 65   Mobile by Alexander Calder. In space-form art, the mobile makes movement a reality. Although this construction is evocative of twigs and leaves in natural
growth, it is also an abstraction to be enjoyed for its loveliness and gaiety. Even in
the photo the shapes seem to float and the structure becomes a living thing. Movement, not a single motion, is complex, the movement in parts related to movement of
the whole. Studying a mobile in motion will awaken the arranger's awareness of the
relationship of form and space.

Courtesy of Museum of Fine Arts, Boston

phasizes that art is never positive. A solution to one problem may not satisfy another.

SPATIAL REVOLUTION

In breaking with tradition, the consideration of space has been an especially strong motivation. Among results in the many "isms" of modern art, the most notable and popular, it seems, are found in Cubism, Futurism, and Non-objectivism. In Cubism, space was thought of as "time" expressed with multi-planned perspective. In life an object or figure changes as it moves in space or as you look at it from different angles. With this in mind, Cubists showed the various factors of a subject as they would be seen from varying positions, but arranged them to blend into one image. In this way the observer could see different time-views simultaneously. Picasso's two-faced figures illustrate.

"Time-motion" in space was the concern in the art movement known as Futurism. Artists overlapped planes in sequence to give an impression of movement in space as would be seen from a stationary position. Although Duchamp was not a futurist painter, his famed *Nude Descending Staircase* is probably the best known work in this style.

Intention in Non-objectivism, of which Mondrian's work is typical, has already been pointed out. You will recall that the interest was simply to divide or organize space with line, shape, and color. Through this as through all the changes in attitude to space, artists were attempting to express or define space without the conventional "window perspective."

In our time, space as an aesthetic problem, is explored in similar veins, but concepts of space take on even greater importance, for new meaning is attached—both factually and philosophically. In this day of atom bombs, jet propulsion, giant structures of steel and glass, science, navigation, all phases of life are affected. It is not possible for the artist to live in our time and keep himself remote from this life and power. More and more we find ideas of motion, of speed, of space transformed to artistic composition. To stimulate aesthetic thinking, a variety of notions exist. A most venturesome one comes from the painter, Soulages, who calls space "a dynamic of the imagination." Another of special challenge is Capogrossi's idea to show men the perspective of space "in which their thoughts move and their actions are born."

Plate 66   Doesn't this composition remind you of delicately carved ivory? Seed heads of wild parsnip are sprayed white and covered with glitter dust. Variegated holly is green and white. Hummel figures are white. Natural voids in the parsnip, like dimensions of pierced space in sculptures by Moore, open up the form so that the eye penetrates to acknowledge depth without looking around it.

Arranger: Mrs. Henry Bircher
Photographer: Howard M. Oberlin

THE SCULPTOR LEADS

But today, sculptors, not painters, take the lead. A reason may be that they have opportunity to define space by manipulating new and varied materials not offered the painter. For example, using transparent plastic, Naum Gabo modeled space without limiting it to opaque form. See Plate 37.

But a greater reason, I believe, is the tangibility of sculpture. It is a touchable, physical structure which offers, it seems, something aesthetically definite and concrete in this day when mankind feels insecure and uncertain in a fast-changing world. This is true even with those sculptures (and there are many) which evoke destructive forces of humanity.

SPECIFIC TRENDS

Among sculptors' conceptions of space it is possible to recognize rather distinct trends. There are those who show their work as a compact self-

Plate 67   *Lobster Trap and Fish Tail* (mobile) by Alexander Calder. The eye finds pleasure and refreshment in constantly changing images; even the changing shadows fascinate the eye. In the hands of an inventive arranger, plants—with their three-dimensional quality and harmonious relationship to each other and to the quality of motion—make highly satisfactory materials for mobiles.

Courtesy of The Museum of Modern Art, New York

contained form extending or breaking out into space, and supported by encompassing void like the Brancusi *Bird In Space*. Then there are those who animate their forms by breaking its solidity into contrasted masses and voids as in the flying mythical *Pegasus* by Lipchitz. Openings are enveloping voids as opposed to penetrating voids, the distinguishing feature of a third trend. In this style solid is punctured with open areas allowing the eye to look through to increase a sense of the sculpture's depth. Henry Moore is immediately associated with this technique not so much because he was the first to use space in this manner, but because the "hole sculptures" have become his hallmark. And still a fourth important trend is represented in sculpture that receives space into its very being. While solid planes enclose space they do not conceal rear features of the structure. In viewing the whole, open volume allows the eye to see within and without simultaneously. *Icon* by Barbara Hepworth exemplifies.

As opposed to these "ground-anchored" types, a fifth trend includes hanging structures. These are mobiles which actually move in space in response to a gust of wind or a gentle push of a hand. Many artists work in this field, but the constructions owe their existence to one man, Alexander Calder, and his awareness of Nature's free motion manifested in such things as falling leaves, moving clouds, stirring water.

A CONCLUSION

In itself, distinction in the use of space may not be important to the layman, but the fact that space in any sense directs artistic activity proves that although a social act, creative art is *of* the time which produces it, not something *from* the time—just as a flower is of the field. Although it is influenced by soil, sunlight and rain, it still has its own root and bloom.

VANGUARD ARRANGERS

In arrangement, as in other fields of art, creativity cannot exist in a vacuum. The arranger, as any artist, moves along with the times. Those who pursue aesthetic revolution of modern abstract techniques will revive an art grown lifeless under a burden of stereotyped design.

But keep in mind that there are degrees of abstraction in art expression; the line between traditional and abstract is somewhat flexible. Each type may take on some quality of the other. It is the dominant quality in a flower arrangement, as in any work of art, that determines classification as to type. Therefore it is important to distinguish the dominant quality in both traditional and abstract techniques. In a broad sense all traditional art tends toward literal representation of a subject portrayed, and assembles design elements to radiate from a static point like petals on a flower, to produce composition which accords with the natural linear perspective; composition takes place within a geometric boundary— pyramid, oval, rectangle, etc. In flower arrangement all this takes form in respect for natural growth properties in plant materials arranged to converge towards one point of radiation to correspond with natural linear perspective, and the whole composed within a preconceived geometric defining boundary.

Abstract art differs in that it departs from natural representation and produces composition in which elements are assembled to suit the designer rather than according to the natural perspective law. And the artist works without a defining boundary in mind. In abstract arrangement natural growth properties are of no importance. Plant materials lose natural associations and become merely the medium for defining space without the use of natural linear perspective. There is no accidental or unplanned element in a composition; every area affects every other area. Resulting interrelationships are rather unexpected and often develop free-form silhouettes—that is, irregular and flowing contours as opposed to those with precise mathematical dimensions; freed from convention the arranger has no predetermined boundary to compose in. It goes without saying, that the further from the natural and conventional a work is, the more abstract it is.

RELATION OF ARRANGEMENT TO ABSTRACTION

It must be pointed out that while abstract art has become the core of anti-naturalism, it is only one aspect of modern art. All abstract arrangements are modern, but not all modern arrangements are abstract. All modern art is distinguished by bold line, shape, form, color, and clean-cut design. It is possible to have these traits in a floral composition and still display the plant materials in accordance with natural appearance, assembling them with interest centered at a common source of radiation. This is traditional designing. Truly modern abstract work is bold and clean-cut to be sure, but arranging technique differs for the assemblage is not unified through interest centered at a one point perspective.

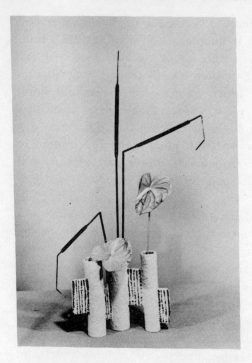

Plate 68   Nature is not art, but in extending it we create new forms and arrive at art. Consider *Praying Mantis* as an experience rather than as an arrangement. In this interpretive-abstract design the unseen (character) extracted from the seen (praying mantis) reveals modern art—bringing out the hidden not the apparent quality of a subject, and fusing it with structure so that one is inseparable from the other. Space supports the various parts, each unit helping to establish unity without a conventionally fixed perspective. In the rhythm of the integrated whole, the definite lines on the container repeat those of the cattails.

Arranger: Mrs. Ernest E. Wunderly
Photographer: Donald C. Huebler

It is this lack of a main focus that is a puzzling and to many an objectionable aspect of modern art. To the uninformed the work of an abstract artist may seem to be nothing but meaningless angles, swirls, and shapes of color and texture. But once we become intimately concerned with what goes into creating *good* abstract design, results appear quite logical and desirable.

Since modern abstract art is not one but many things, to understand it the arranger must find the common denominator in works which are classed abstract. Analyzing numerous examples drawn from various fields of art brings to light that *simplified characterization* is the common quality. A double check is that this satisfies the dictionary definition of the term abstract. According to this authoritative source, the verb means "to draw from; to separate a quality from a thing to which it belongs."

In art, we abstract by separating the *important* from the *unimportant*. This tends to emphasize essential factors or character of a subject, and results in *simplified characterization*.

As an adjective Mr. Webster defines abstract as "expressing a quality apart from any object that possesses it; a quality separately considered."

Plate 69   Working unconvention-
ally with even numbers, the arranger has used elements not to
present plant materials in a container but as space delineators of
line, shape, form, color, and texture, producing decorative-abstract
composition to satisfy her design
concept. And we see the materials
in this relation, rather than as dried
yarrow, papyrus, and container.
As in traditional technique, line does
not taper the eye into surrounding
space. Instead it ends in bold eye-
catching form. Nor is there the
traditional concentration of interest
in one area. Balance and unity are
achieved through timing which
spreads interest in a balanced relationship over the entire design. In
analysis the eye sees the parallel
shapes simultaneously. Pause points
fairly close together low in the pattern retain the eye with force
enough to counteract that of the
high area to which the eye moves
rapidly by means of the large space
interval.

Arranger: Kathryn Holley Seibel
Photographer: William E. Seibel

In designing this means using an element of line, shape, form, color, texture for nothing more than because it is line, shape, form, color, texture.
Applied to arrangement, plant material is selected because of certain
elements it possesses rather than because it is a flower, a fruit, a leaf, a
branch. For example, the arranger selects a branch not as a branch of a
tree, but as a line with straightness or curviness, thickness or thinness,
smoothness or roughness, and with directional shape which when combined with other lines and shapes, will create a form structure governed
by the arranger's personal feeling for design. Aware of Cézanne's innova-
tion that color is more than decorative, the arranger does not think of

color, and texture as well, as something *on* a form, but that it *is* the form. A chrysanthemum, for instance, is not categorized a flower, but a colored sphere with a touch quality of texture. That an apple is the fruit of a tree is not reason for its use; shape, form, color, texture is. Quality, you see, is separately considered as the dictionary definition dictates. In abstract attitude the arranger separates the important qualities (shape, form, color, texture) from the unimportant (the fact that they are products of Nature).

In all abstract arrangement, the artist is interested in plant material only in so far as it affects his sense of space; he completely dismisses from his mind the physical identity of his medium. Once we realize that lines, shapes, forms, areas of color and texture may stand alone as essential character representing the utmost economy of means, we have a clue to the purest kind of abstract arrangement.

STRUCTURAL UNITY

Since the parts of a pure abstract design are not united by the physical tie of a center of interest they are more or less isolated in space, not submerged in the finished composition as happens to a great extent in traditional technique. Line as it moves upward does not necessarily taper to release the eye to surrounding area; it might very well end in bold eye-catching form if it suits the arranger's design concept. But the arrangement nevertheless is organized so that the finished structure can be seen whole; it must not be viewed fragmentarily. The revolt of the abstractionist is anti-tradition, not anti-order. In fact, since he is completely freed from the formula of man-made rule, he is led to experiment and so requires an especially thorough grounding in principles if his arrangement is to be unified.

Unification of the separated shapes into structural oneness is accomplished through eye control. In traditional arrangement the eye is first drawn to a center of interest. From here it moves through the composition returning to this area where it may begin again the rhythmic experience of following a "line of continuity." But in abstract technique the eye does not find such a magnet of unity as a starting point. The eye may begin its path anywhere, but passage through the composition must be an easy one nevertheless. The problem becomes one of purposeful placing of elements in space. To fuse aspects of Nature, of feeling, of imagination, requires complete control of one's medium. The various area units because of shape, color, or texture, exert different influences on the eye and on the other shapes in the design, so the arranger must relate each unit so that if one is moved, the uniting rhythm of easy eye path (line of continuity) is destroyed; every unit is vital to every other unit and to the whole of mass and space.

From earlier discussion you will recall that the eye may be controlled by means of repetition, directional shapes, force of color and texture areas, and spacing. Space intervals speed up or slow down eye movement depending on the need to balance tension areas throughout the composition. We can think of each separate tension area as a pause point momentarily holding the eye. If there is need to have the eye linger in one section of the design so that in visual balance this part will compensate for something more forceful elsewhere, space intervals narrow down between the pause points. The closer together areas are spaced, the slower the eye movement will be; the farther apart, the faster the eye will move. With this attention to timing, interest is spread all over the composition, not centered at one main area.

SPACE ASSUMES IMPORTANCE

In abstract arrangement, as in other abstract art forms, space assumes greater importance than it does in traditional work. Voids are never left to chance; they are planned as the arranger places his solids in position, to function beyond the conventional aid to pleasing silhouette. The artist of abstract technique is definitely a space planner. He considers negative space as a positive element; space shape (negative space) is every bit as important as the shape of solid (positive space). Actually, like the sculptor, the abstract arranger models space with his solids. He uses space not only to support the various parts of a composition and to bind the forms together through eye control, but to invite the eye to adventure into hollows and around swellings, to see within the structure, through it, and between the parts. Planned void within the structure itself goes far in preventing an effect of flatness, a tendency when a minimum of material is used, as happens in abstract work where *every* area plays a vital role. Careful spacing from front to back gives depth planes to in-

Plate 70   A daring composition with no subject but its own design. The relationship of abstract shape, form, and color relies on a new way of seeing—the intermixing of solid and space. The sensitive use of these elements would be apparent to one who would attempt to vary the position of units or add something to the relationship. Components are split dark green cycas leaves with rigid and pointed segments, a black modern bowl on its side, and four diamond-shaped boards, two in orange lacquer, two in black.

Arranger: Mrs. William Wheeler
Photographer: William Sevecke

crease three-dimensional quality. Furthermore, with space used positively, arrangements have pleasing contours from any angle; parts are tied together and yet seem free—almost as if they had the capacity to move.

With all this concern with planned space, voids in abstract arrangement are not *in* the arrangement as they are apt to be in traditional work, but *of* the arrangement, as the vase's opening is *of* the vase. In traditional composition we lose this space—so much a part of our container—when we bring plant material over the lip, often completely concealing it. The designer interested in abstract technique would unify vase and plant forms by relating the openness of the container to the openness in the design, making the material an integrated part of the container. The result is a total experience of an art form, not flowers in a vase.

THE TOTAL WHOLE

And the container is not a subordinated factor as it is in traditional arranging where the vase or bowl is just an instrument holding plant mate-

Plate 71   An artist arranger does not renounce the old because it is old, nor use the new because it is new; he finds something of the present in each. Concept, design, and technique merge in this "free-style" holiday composition using red poinsettias and green ti leaves. Although abstract quality is considered in the rolled leaves, they are combined with plant material in its natural state, with the conventional center of interest to unify. In the background, however, the arranger goes completely modern with an abstract "window" inspired by stained-glass windows of the modernist, Marc Chagall. This is a collage of clippings from world-wide newspapers—a most suitable backdrop against which to present her subject, *Joy to the World—Here, There, and Everywhere*. Unfortunately, in the photograph, the newspaper print is not clearly visible.

Arranger: Mrs. Saul Shapiro
Photographer: A. L. Armitage

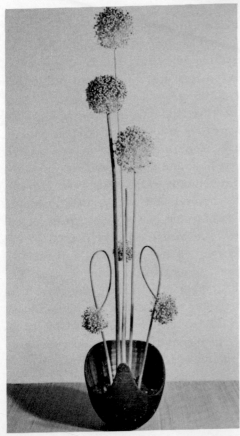

Plate 72   To call this an arrangement of allium misses the point, for it is used as abstract line and form (simplified characterization) in imaginative design concept, and the spectator is not called upon to read into it anything other than simple elements of line and point which, with an element of unique form (the container), are organized in space. Unity is achieved by eye passage controlled through repetition, direction, and space interval rather than by skeleton convergence. Note how openness in the design of points and lines relates to the opening in the modern container designed by Harry Schulke, with full integration a result. Duality is resolved through a dominantly centered vertical rhythm.

Arranger: Kathryn Holley Seibel
Photographer: William E. Seibel

rial to show off its external beauty. In abstract arranging the container may dominate with plant forms used in subordination to point up its form and pattern. In abstract work even a plaque if it is an especially lovely one, need not play a subordinate role. Too figures are *never* accessories as the traditional arranger thinks of them.

Just as structural supports are often left exposed as integrated solids in the design of modern architecture, so they are in abstract arrangement. A support to elevate a portion of the composition, for example, would become a visual part of that composition. Even the structural support of a pinholder need not be concealed. If it is planned as an important shape (possibly painted to fit the color plan), it will not be unsightly in the overall concept. It goes without saying, however, that any foundation unit must be attractive enough to stand exposure. *The thing to remember is that no unit, no part of an abstract design is necessarily more important than any other; every unit is just a solid in space.*

SELECTION ALL-IMPORTANT

All this makes it clear that a directive in abstract designing stems from the contention that "art form (the total whole) evolves from the material." In our medium practically everything in Nature can be employed as pure abstractions. Purely abstract shapes are easy to find—apples are ball-shapes; cattails are cylinders; tulips are oval shapes; lilies are cones; etc. It might seem from what has been said that the abstractionist arranger regards line, shape, and areas of color and texture as ends in themselves. Not at all. Line, shape, form, areas of color, and texture, are the tangible elements. These are basic and primary and very often the inspiration for design, but the abstractionist learns to see these elements as something *different* from the natural and always *subordinate* to imaginative artistic end. Psychological factors play a large part in successful work. In other words, interest in the visual aspect or natural growth pattern of plant material so important to the traditionalist is replaced by interest in the *nature* or *character* of its growth, its *living force*. The abstractionist feels the rhythmic *strength* of a branch, the *grace* with which a flower carries its head, the *falling* movement of pendulous bloom, the *springing vigor* of grasses. In the awareness of a design force in his medium he utilizes Nature rather than conforms to it as does the traditionalist who strives to show off the *visual* beauty of plant material.

Plate 73   To interpret the formal pattern of a Lombardy poplar, spathiphyllum foliage was chosen because of shape association; its leaf suggests the silhouette of the poplar. Reversing usual practice, largest shapes are at the top, smallest toward the base. This shows both full view and sides of the tree's elliptical form rather like a Picasso portrait in which profile and full face are shown simultaneously. In other words, the composition is conceived from reality of conception rather than from reality of vision. The exposed pinholder adds to rather than detracts from the design; it serves as a stabilizing factor in the perpendicular balance; at the same time the supporting pins repeat the pattern created by the leaf stems.

Arranger: Mrs. William S. Carper
Photographer: Stan Sheets

EXPERIENCING MATERIAL

To become more alert to the meaning of abstract qualities and to become more sensitive to possibilities, it is helpful to examine plant shapes in varied positions. Examine the simple shape of a palm boot, for instance. Study its back view as well as the front; see it in profile. Hold it in both vertical and horizontal position above and below eye level. Note its pattern in diagonal position with both ends free in space (possible in arrangement when given elevating support). Face the shape toward the light and away from it to see modulations of light and dark values to stimulate interest. When involved this way with abstract quality do not say, "This is a palm boot." This would be communicating a fact but would not convey any feeling. Instead call it a shape modifier and modulator. This is experiencing the shape emotionally rather than intellectually.

LIBERTY ACCORDED

Free from tradition the arranger's imagination often leads to finding ways to cause flowers and leaves to lose their natural identity and thus increase the abstract quality. For example, blooms arranged in close proximity, one against the other, produce abstract line that can be directed in straight paths or curves, even spiralled around an object. Sometimes arrangers are interested in creating totally new forms. One practice is to cut off the bloom and use just the flower's stem, or to remove petals and use the center of a flower as abstract form. A *part* of a leaf is usable—in heavy foliage perhaps the center rib or an intriguing vein structure, the flesh having been carefully cut away. Knotting strap-like leaves, even braiding them, forges new images out of familiar ones— you will think of other possibilities as the need arises in your work.

In abstract constructions, Cubists added textures to their canvases. This could be done in flower arrangement. For instance, the adding of cloves to an orange or apple could be as representative of modern abstract art—if used with regard to shape and form—as it is typical of the old-fashioned, functional pomander ball. When these abstract pomanders have become dried they are amazingly light in weight and would be interesting possibilities for mobiles which many find so irresistible.

Color as well as texture adds abstract quality. Kandinsky, an acknowl-edged leader among abstract painters, used color to create mood values, not to suggest an original object. This arbitrary use of color—abstract color—is typical of many of the modern painters. There was the wild ex-aggeration of hue by Van Gogh who used so much more yellow and blue than in the model; the decorative use of soft violets, pinks, and greens with little regard for the way things occurred in Nature by Gauguin; and the shrieking color contrasts combined into unified composition by Matisse, perhaps the greatest colorist of all. Just how far Paul Klee pushed his experiments with color is vividly illustrated in *Senecio*, a round head with eyes, nose, mouth, and Adam's apple suggested by the simplest of geometric shapes. At first glance the figure seems static, but as you look at it, the face becomes a moving thing with red eyes seeming to roll in their sockets, and blue-pink cheeks to push forward because of the color behind. It is the dynamics of color that gives the illusion far more than shapes and arrangement. Yellow and pink are soft hues and become even more so due to a surrounding orange of darker value. But behind this softness one senses a characterization of awkward shyness.

For all the moderns, color is a tool for achieving characterization. In this vein, arrangers are often led to distort plant material with paint or dye. Even a naturalistic figure when given a coat of untrue color takes on a degree of abstract character for it conceals natural detail. Is there anyone unfamiliar with the "Purple Cow?" A creature so treated loses some association with the natural—is de-naturalized we might say, and so presents abstraction to some extent.

Because the abstractionist arranger is not interested in natural appearances, to disguise naturalistic aspect of flowers and leaves can increase the impact and urgency of the artist's intent, but distortion is effective only when it has meaning for the design. *A word of caution:* Avoid changing forms for the sake of distortion or deformation; such liberty is conceded only if it has compositional benefit, or to deepen the expressive or emotional quality. The abstract arranger must have total effect in mind in his use of plant materials. To avoid bizarre results, use your freedom constructively, not just for novelty.

The fact that for years arrangers have been curling leaves, rolling their tips, and in other ways changing the physical identity of plant material, reveals that abstract quality in flower arrangement is not a sudden development. But until arrangers began to emphasize abstraction, any distorted plant life was combined with a predominance of material in its natural state, all radiating from a common source within a preconceived geometric boundary. It is accurate to call such work "modern-traditional" or "free-style."

SEEING THINGS INWARDLY

In the search for essence, spirit, simplified characterization of a subject, its personal appeal, learn to look beneath the surface of things. Seeing them inwardly, you will detect an underlying character in the impression you get. You can find such characterization in every subject whether an object as a flower, an emotion as joy, a mood as excitement, or an idea as hardship. For analysis I select *bird* as subject matter. Seeing inwardly, I feel *flight* to be the significant character and the thing to be stressed. Flight then, becomes my inspiration. Reducing the idea to its simplest form, I visualize a long tapering shape diagonally poised to "shoot" through space. This impression is what architect Frank Lloyd Wright would describe as "the graphic soul of the thing." This is definitely abstracting, for the diagonal direction is a sensory symbol, an effect, if you will, far removed from a natural picture of something in flight. To carry out my impression of an extended linear shape as basic to the natural form of a bird in flight, I would wire together two long coconut spathes at the stem ends to produce a single compact form tapering to a point at the extremities. With this anchored in diagonal position on a tall aluminum rod I would have a visual counterpart of my impression, with elevation reinforcing the theme of flight. With semi-gloss paint (shine to increase a sense of smoothness), I would paint the sheaths' convex outer surfaces gray, their concave inner surfaces, gray-blue. Distance and space would thus be evoked, for grayed color is unobtrusive to the eye, releasing it easily to surrounding space. A grouping of blue hydrangea blooms where the spathes join would not only conceal unattractive mechanics, but add to the expressive function of color. The flowers could be kept fresh with water-soaked Oasis packed into the hollow where the spathes are joined as one. Color, direction, and elevation would work together to heighten a feeling of unrestricted, atmospheric space, with composition a direct and economical statement expressing the *essence* of my previsualized theme, a flying bird.

Like this conception, the shape patterns in Figure 16 (a and f) reveal simplified characterization of flight, not a visual likeness. For every suggestion, dozens of substitutes are possible, for an individual's manner of seeing and feeling is a personal thing greatly influenced by the sum total of his life's experiences.

In arrangement the final structure relates not only to the designer's personal reaction to the subject (whether the subject is a theme in interpretive work or just composition in decorative arrangement), but to the material available, and to the space allotted the arrangement. But in any case, because only essentials are selected and emphasized (the unseen abstracted from the seen), simplified characterization results.

REALISM VS. NATURALISM

It is apparent that to abstract is to refine and to refine is to intensify and condense. But let it be understood that rejection of naturalistic association does not result in work that lacks reality; it cannot be classed as artificial. To the contrary, it strengthens reality. In expressing something beyond visual experience, we are perhaps driving the arrangement art to its extreme, but it definitely produces compositions spurred by Nature toward expression charged with reality. In the discourse on interpretive arrangement, Chapter VI, it was determined that although results of subjective expression are not naturalistic, they are *realistic*. They are realistic in the sense of characterization. In other words, realism of physical identity of a subject (representation; surface reality) is replaced with realism of character (abstraction; inner reality). The arranger has taken into account the inner reality of the phenomena around him, that he may employ Nature as a more effective tool in artistic expression. In the end the arranger uses his knowledge and understanding of the real toward a more complete and truer interpretation.

The same is true of abstract-decorative arrangement for this too is subjectively motivated. Through the designer's penetrating eye he has felt the very nature of things. His work may be inspired by Nature's governing laws—the shape of form, the perpetual action of the ocean waves, the unfolding of plants, the play of light, color effect, etc., and he will combine plant forms, taking advantage of their inner reality to strengthen his design concept, guided always by *feeling*—not an emotional feeling of joy, of peace, and such, but an artistic feeling.

USING A FAMILIAR SYMBOL

Significantly, the rising interest in abstraction reveals growth in arrangement, and this is good, for things are at low ebb unless they are growing. However, departure from literal representation which is the very heart of abstract art does not completely reject all familiar factor—an iron link in an interpretation of strength, for example, or a chunk of glass slag suggesting ice to convey an impression of coldness. The arranger can use such things to aid in achieving illusions, much as Calder did in his *Clouds Over the Mountain*. You cannot miss his large steel peak-shaped "mountains" nor the platelike "clouds," but these are not imitations of nature's forms. Like the glass slag "ice," they are metaphors. And the iron link is a symbol, not representative. Metaphors and symbols have appeal in their familiar aspect. The love of the familiar is inherent in humanity and too, the familiar supplies a key of recognition to the audience.

ABSTRACTION AND CREATIVITY

Theory and practice of abstraction is stimulating and thought provoking, and gives satisfaction to the creative drive within the artist. Any arrangement predominantly abstract is subjective in inspiration, is of the *self*, it comes from the artist's insight rather than from a visual sight. Then too, the more abstraction a work possesses the more it demands the viewer's imagination, and therefore his participation. The composition becomes not just artistic form, but a truly communicative force. Viewer's response to abstract art is covered in the following chapter.

Art should and must reflect its time. In our twentieth century world, there is no creative medium which has not undergone revolution or evolution—if flower arrangement is an art form, it cannot be different. This is an age of adventure and exploration for the arranger as for the artist in any other sphere. Abstract flower arrangement rather than being rebellious should be an art of growth; it is a consciousness of possibilities. At its best it represents a deeper understanding of the art's evolution and cultivation. Life itself is change and growth; abstract designing enables arrangers to live up to this philosophy in flower arrangement.

The keys to abstract art given here are offered with only a brief explanation of historical and philosophical ideas that led modern artists into various ways of working in abstraction. In themselves these are enlightening and worthy of serious research. The challenge is left with you.

VIII RESPONSE AND APPRAISAL

VIEWER'S RESPONSE

Since abstraction is a process of seeing, it involves a change in seeing habits for the viewer as well as for the artist. The artist creates a design and the viewer responds to his work—both are taking part in the eye's revolution. Because the non-objective work will lack the emotional intensity of abstract-expressionism, it is generally less appreciated by the public, and yet to the initiated reveals its soundness and worthiness. But just how can the observer respond to such work? And to abstract-expressionism when withdrawl from the natural is so complete that there is no evidence of a subject per se?

Intelligent response can only be gained by readjustments of thinking procedures. As far as the artist is concerned, let it be realized that he cares little or nothing about what the viewer thinks of his work or how he responds to it. He is expressing something vital to his own thinking, to his own attitude in relation to the world around him. It is even possible that his work reflects a happening which only he has encountered.

Understanding this, one who looks at abstract composition should not attempt to find a theme, nor ask what does the work mean? This does not imply, however, that it will be without meaning to him. Quite

151

the contrary, for abstraction can involve him in new experiences. He can respond more fully and more fervently to the language of form and color than is possible in traditional work where intention is to portray plant material as a product of Nature rather than as a relationship of shapes, forms, color, and texture.

PSYCHOLOGICAL REACTION

The viewer's response is much a matter of seeing emotionally. If elements have been wisely chosen, well related, and carefully integrated, the fused value experienced in the total whole incites psychological response in the viewer. Reaction to the shapes in space is not a matter of superficial seeing, but of feeling, a deeper seeing. This becomes a plastic experience, for with his mind and his imagination, the viewer *feels* their movement, their forces. In abstract art the observer enters a world that is strange to him for the work is not what it is, but what it might be; not what it is as an image, but what it is as feeling. The composition has meaning for the viewer only in relation to his life's experiences. And his experience need not match that which motivated the artist's work. It may be one of many things—strength, elegance, grace, warmth, even violence. A concrete example is helpful. You can experience a strong psychological impact in the arrangement, Plate 69. The papyrus and yarrow are so much more than plant material; within their narrow limits there is design force with movement upward. The container serves to point this up for in itself it holds the same force. In the recurring parallelism of upward direction in shapes, one experiences the impression of stateliness. To appreciate the composition's abstract quality the observer forgets that the vertical rectangular form is a container and the other elements are plant material—all was chosen because of a harmony of shape, color, and texture with enough variety to give vitality to the arrangement. It is the coalescence of all contributing components that the observer experiences in the impact of stateliness.

JUDGE AS VIEWER

What relates to the viewer's appraisal of abstract arrangement applies, of course, to one who serves as judge of competitive work. The purely abstract design is a comparatively new event for him. Loosened from conventional moorings it is in danger of being misunderstood by the judge unless he, like the arranger, continues to grow with the times, and like the abstract designer, establishes new ways to see and think. Abstractionism is still in an experimental stage; it requires time to prove itself. During the interim, bizarre—even ugly—designs are bound to be displayed. But there will be beautiful arrangements too, for surely good designers will continue to make good arrangements.

WHAT THE JUDGE LOOKS FOR

Just as he does in evaluating traditional arrangement, a judge of abstract composition considers the arranger's respect for principles in his assemblage of elements, and takes into account his attention to pleasing contours, surface texture and color which give aesthetic satisfaction. He notes too, a worthy utilization of space to develop a three-dimensional art form. But he sees the arrangement differently for there will be no stereotyped pattern or "image-cliché" to accord with conventional unification toward a common point of radiation.

It is inevitable that abstract composition brings into being new values and standards of judgment. The judge no longer visualizes the arrangement as something which occupies empty space. He sees it as something which models active space and so the one is a part of the other. Void and mass cannot be separated in the judge's appraisal. This is true even if to convey a sense of power, the arranger has accented solidity in a compact design; if solid and space are one, as they should be, the solid will seem to push out into the space.

In line with this the judge dismisses from his mind the identity of an arrangement's ingredients. What the container is, and what the plant material is, or how it grows, accounts for little of the impact the design has on him. Like the exhibitor, he is concerned with relationships. He sees the areas for what they are in line, shape, form, color, and texture related to each other with respect for space, direction, movement, force, and color tonality. His final scoring is dependent on the designer's skill in using the abstract qualities of his medium to best advantage.

The judge recognizes an economy of material and a simplicity in the execution of the arrangement. He has always known the value of simplicity, but abstraction introduces him to new experiences in simplicity. With a mutual relationship between occupying form and the space which contains it, compositions are streamlined, often with the impact of contrast due to little or no transitional material.

JUDGING ABSTRACT COMPOSITIONS

Since response to abstract art is psychological, it is seeing emotionally as it were, and has nothing to do with seeing a definite story-telling theme. Decorative arrangement—that is, arrangement planned to beautify its setting—can be classed as non-objective, so the judge does not expect the work to have been inspired by a theme. There may be one, however, because decorative and interpretive character often overlap, but in the scoring of decorative work, a theme-subject would be inconsequential. Responsive impact for the judge comes from pure design relationship, not story-telling quality. The design itself, is the subject and is what is important to the judge of decorative-abstract arrangement; he is not concerned with expressive content.

If it is interpretive work that is being considered for an award, then of course content is recognized as a major factor. In this classification the judge should base his estimate on how well the exhibitor has related abstract elements of design to give concrete form to a simplified characterization of the theme-subject.

Since the abstract expressionist arranger works with a world we cannot see, he extracts the unseen from the seen, and the *unseen* becomes his inspiration. More often than not, the arranger will so distill his theme, that only he would be able to name the original source of his abstraction. For this reason it is imperative that the arranger's inspiration accompany his flower show entry in all interpretive classes; that the judge knows the subject given on the schedule is not enough. For detailed analysis of this particular problem I refer you to pages 24-25 in *Giving and Getting Awards for Flower Arrangement* published by Hearthside Press, Inc. Risking reproach by some, I maintain it a disadvantage to schedule definite subjects for interpretive-abstract classes in a flower show. However the notion displeases the schedule designer, the ideal situation is complete freedom for the exhibitor apart from fitting his choice into the overall theme of the show. A parallel would be a photographer's choice of a subject for a general theme because it inspired him as opposed to a subject assigned to him.

In any case, the judge must not overlook the fact that in expressive work, the artist's inspiration is more important than the subject being interpreted. So to fully appreciate the expressionist's concept he must know what qualities the exhibitor extracted from the subject to emphasize as his personal reaction.

SUBJECT AND CONTENT

Sometimes *subject* and *content* are confused. We must remember that subject may be nothing more than *composition;* content is *expressiveness* which is the expression of the designer's personal reaction to a storytelling subject, a *theme,* in other words.

CRITICAL EVALUATION

Evaluating the actual execution of the arrangement boils down to looking for mutual relationship between mass and space (never detail), strong sculptural solids with voids, or powerful meaningful masses which break into surrounding space, contours attractive from any angle, easy eye passage throughout the arrangement with the eye refreshed with rest areas (pause points) as it is directed onward by balanced interest.

In judging, one should look at the abstract composition as an experience, not as a flower arrangement. Toward this the eyes should "wander" over the whole without seeing the individual units, being aware only of pattern. This becomes an easy matter by looking through half-closed eye lids to put the eyes deliberately out of focus, blurring individual parts.

It is only after the judge experiences the arrangement as a whole and determines if it is stimulating or merely a static collection of shapes, that he is ready for critical evaluation. If the combination of elements appears to be without purpose, the judge should look for the cause in one of three things, or in any combination of the three: *selection, relationship, integration.*

CONSTRUCTIVE COMMENT

After the judge checks all contributing factors suggested by a scale of points, he determines if some adjustment in the composition would heighten design effectiveness without adding other kinds of material or other relationships. Constructive criticism relates to increasing design force not to changing the exhibitor's concept. A judge must remember that whatever the concept, it is right for the one who has it, no matter how it may differ from his own. Since visual likeness to any subject is absent, the judge is free to disagree with, even dislike the exhibitor's portrayal of a theme. When expressive content is intended, and the judge is aware of the inspiration behind the work, his obligation is merely to estimate how understandable the exhibitor has made this— what it happens to be is not the problem. Only when this takes place will there be an active delight in judging, not a mere tolerance of something the judge cares nothing about.

ABSTRACT ARRANGEMENT RATES HIGH

Should a schedule fail to designate the type of arrangement expected, it is possible that work in both traditional and abstract styles will be represented in a single class. If in such a situation there is a traditional and an abstract entry equally well designed for its type, which would be accredited with the first award? It must be kept in mind that abstract composition is not a superior kind of design; it is only the lastest development of art as a whole. Can you say which fragrance is the better—the perfume of a single rose, or the scent from a rose arbor? And so it is with arrangement. We cannot say one kind is better than another just because it covers another phase. But on the other hand, abstract arrangement is more difficult to do well than the traditional. Because it requires greater restraint and greater precision in placing the solids in space, abstract work does not allow for mistakes. Then too abstract art is more creative than traditional. Remember it is creation not alone for the arranger but for the observer too—for the artist through subjective expression; for the observer through response in him that the well designed abstract arrangement evokes. In view of these considerations, well executed abstract work rates higher than traditional arrangement which at best represents objective, not subjective, expression.

A JUDGE'S OBLIGATION

Revolutionary art forms are rarely considered good design by judges trained to evaluate only traditional arrangements. For this reason a contemporary judge worthy of the title is obligated to become familiar with abstract art even if he cannot find it in his heart to like it. This is a must for there is one thing that is certain—he will be finding more and more abstract exhibits in competitive flower shows. Because abstract technique supplies freedom in designing, it propels arrangement activity into unparalleled opportunity for creativity, and becomes a real challenge; the truly creative arranger cannot escape it. Is it too much to expect the judge of abstract arrangement to develop at least as much interest in abstract designing as the exhibitor? Indeed, he cannot afford to do otherwise.

A PARTING WORD

In conclusion let it be remembered that it is a privilege granted to man to be creative, and to know the abiding and satisfying joy of creation. For the arranger, the art of looking is the root of the whole problem. Without the ability to perceive deeply he is without the stimulus to create. A penetrating vision is his source of power.

Remember that whatever happens to you as a person affects you as a creative arranger. Your work differs from earlier attempts because of something that occurred physically, emotionally, mentally—even a realization of the place of art in your life would have influence.

As for the judge, to approach judging with open mind, and to explore arrangement with an appreciative rather than a critical eye, is what marks her service valuable to the exhibitor, arrangers, and the public.

The search for broader vision on the part of both arranger and judge means new life and growth for flower arrangement. And in the search it behooves all to hold in mind words penned by Ralph Waldo Emerson—they are worth remembering:

> "In the vaunted works of Art
> The master-stroke is Nature's Part."

This leads to greater appreciation for all art which in turn leads us back to Nature with sharper eye, a witness to the fact that Nature, Man, and Art can meet on common ground.

So much more could be said; there is much to discover for yourself which you can tuck away in your subconscious to be drawn upon when required. But more important, you will have a thrilling relationship with that wonderful thing we call Nature.

INDEX

158